T0361189

Israel

First published in 1985, this study, focusing on Israel, looks at the under-lying reasons why certain political, economic and social events have taken place in the country's history. It provides vital analysis of the political and economic issues of the country, and those that have affected it, as well as providing statistical material on all the key data of the political economy.

The book was originally published as part of the Middle East Research Insti-tute (MERI) Reports on the Middle East which quickly established them-selves as the most authoritative and up-to-date information on the state of affairs in the region.

Israel

MERI Report

Middle East Research Institute

First published in 1985
by Croom Helm

This edition first published in 2015 by Routledge
2 Park Square, Milton Park, Abingdon, Oxon, OX14 4RN
and by Routledge
711 Third Avenue, New York, NY 10017

Routledge is an imprint of the Taylor & Francis Group, an informa business

Publisher's Note
The publisher has gone to great lengths to ensure the quality of this reprint but points out that some imperfections in the original copies may be apparent.

Disclaimer
The publisher has made every effort to trace copyright holders and welcomes correspondence from those they have been unable to contact.

A Library of Congress record exists under LC control number: 85004164

ISBN 13: 978-1-138-90212-1 (hbk)
ISBN 13: 978-1-315-69754-3 (ebk)

MERI REPORT

ISRAEL

Middle East Research Institute
University of Pennsylvania

CROOM HELM
London • Sydney • Dover, New Hampshire

© 1985 Middle East Research Institute
Croom Helm Ltd, Provident House, Burrell Row,
Beckenham, Kent BR3 1AT

Croom Helm Australia Pty Ltd, First Floor,
139 King Street, Sydney, NSW 2001, Australia

British Library Cataloguing in Publication Data .

Israel. — (MERI report)
  1. Israel
  I. MERI II. Series
  956.94'054   DS126.5

  ISBN 0-7099-3548-X

Croom Helm, 51 Washington Street, Dover,
New Hampshire 03820, USA

Library of Congress Cataloging in Publication Data
applied for.

TABLE OF CONTENTS

I. Background

II. Political Analysis

IV. Statistical Appendix

Defense

Economy

Demography

Budget.

Energy

Industry and Agriculture

Trade

Labor

Transportation and Communication

Health, Education and Welfare

I. BACKGROUND

1. GEOGRAPHY. Israel is located at the eastern end of the Mediterranean Sea. It is bordered to the north by Lebanon, to the northeast by Syria, to the east and southeast by Jordan, to the southwest by Egypt and to the west by the Mediterranean.

Israel's pre-1967 area is 20,255 sq km of land (1 sq km = 0.386 sq mi) and 445 sq km of inland water. The area of the occupied and annexed territories total 7,407 sq km comprising the West Bank (5,879), Gaza (378), East Jerusalem (70), and the Golan Heights (1,150). The annexation of East Jerusalem in 1967 and the Golan Heights in 1981 have not been internationally recognized. The geographical area comprised by Israel, the West Bank, and Gaza is divided into four natural regions: (1) the Mediterranean coastal plain (Israel and Gaza); (2) the central highlands; (3) the Jordan Rift Valley (Israel and the West Bank); and (4) the Negev Desert (Israel). The central highlands, averaging 610 m, reach their highest point at Mt. Miron (1 m = 3.28 ft).

The Jordan River is the principal drainage system. Originating in the Dan, Hasbani, and Banias rivers, it flows into the freshwater Sea of Galilee and terminates in the highly saline Dead Sea, the lowest point on earth at 400 m below sea level. There are two much smaller rivers, the Yarkon and the Kishon, that empty into the Mediterranean, and a small section of the Yarmuk, a tributary of the Jordan River.

The most populous region is the coastal plain, where most of the Israeli population is concentrated in large urban centers and where the Gaza Strip Palestinians have one of the highest population densities in the world. In the central highlands, only Jerusalem and its environs have a substantial Israeli Jewish population. The largest concentration of Israeli Arabs lives in the Galilee in the northern portion of the highlands. Further south lies the West Bank, with its archipelago of Palestinian villages, a dozen principle towns, and a scattering of Israeli settlements. The Jordan Rift Valley and the Negev Desert are sparsely populated.

2. CLIMATE. The climate is governed by Israel's location between the subtropical arid zone prevailing in Egypt to the south, and the subtropical wet zone prevailing in Lebanon to the north. The climate is Mediterranean; the coldest month is January at 5 to 10° C (40-50° F) and the hottest month is August at 18 to 38° C (65-100° F). Substantial rainfall occurs only during the five month period from November to March and is unevenly distributed in the country. In the south, the rainfall is light, averaging less than 100 mm annually (1 mm = 0.039 in), while in the north, average annual rainfall is 1,128 mm. The areas most cultivated are those that receive more than 300 mm a year; these include the coastal plain, the Jezreel Valley, the northern part of the Jordan Valley, and the Galilee.

3. POPULATION. At the end of 1983, the population of Israel was 4,200,000 (including 12,000 Syrian Druze in the Golan Heights which was annexed in 1982). The Israeli Jewish population was about 3.4 million, the Muslims nearly 600,000, Christians about 90,000, while Druze and others were about 50,000. In addition, there were an estimated 704,000 Palestinian Arabs in the West Bank, (including Jerusalem) and 420,000 in the Gaza Strip.

Two factors have historically affected population growth in Israel. An irregular growth pattern resulted from the several waves of immigration. The first from 1948-1951, involved primarily Europeans and Jews from neighboring Arab countries, while the second, from 1955-1957 and the third from 1961-1964 included immigrants from Eastern Europe, North Africa and the Middle East. Since then, the number of immigrants has been relatively low, primarily from the USA and the USSR from 1971-1980.

The second factor is the differential rate of Jewish and non-Jewish population increase. The annual growth rate for the population in 1982 was 1.7 percent. The growth rate of the Jewish population was 1.4 percent, while the non-Jewish population grew by 3 percent. The lower growth rate of the Jewish population as compared to the Arabs is due to a lower birth rate (25 Jewish births per thousand population as compared to 34 for Arabs), a low level of immigration (13,500), and emigration estimated tentatively at 7,400. Long-term projections, assuming medium conditions of Jewish and Arab fertility and Jewish immigration/emigration, predict that the proportion of Jewish population will by 2010 decrease to 75 percent. If the administered territories are annexed, Jews will by 2010 become a clear minority, comprising 45 percent of the overall population. This prospect is also reflected in the age structure of the population; the average age of the Jewish population is 30.4, as compared with the non-Jewish average at 20.7 years.

In recent years, there has been a growing concern over the "brain drain" of young, Ashkenazi, educated, white collar workers leaving Israel permanently. Although it is difficult to estimate their numbers, some have claimed that from 1948 until 1983, from 350,000 to 500,000 have emigrated abroad, primarily toward the USA and Europe.

4. RESOURCES. Israel is poor in natural resources. Mineral resources include potash, bromine and magnesium in the Dead Sea. Mining of phosphate rock in the Negev reached 2,085,000 metric tons in 1979. Copper ore, which is mined in the Arava, reached 8,000 metric tons in 1975 and declined subsequently. Small amounts of oil and natural gas are found in the Negev; annual production was estimated in 1979 at 150,960 bbl, amounting to just 1-2 percent of total consumption. Large deposits of oil shale have been discovered and may become an important source of energy in the future.

Electric power is mainly generated from thermal stations. Production of electricity reached 11,874 million kwh towards the end of the 1970s. Because local fuel is scarce, the government sponsors extensive research into alternative energy sources. The Atomic Energy Commission, established in 1952, has two research facilities; it is laying the groundwork for a number of atomic power stations, the first of which is scheduled to be built in the 1980s.

5. SOCIAL STRUCTURE. In terms of social structure, there are marked differences according to ethnic origin. Whereas approximately 65 percent of the Ashkenazim concentrate in white collar occupations, 55 percent of the Sephardim are found in the blue collar stratum. While the second generation (native born) Sephardi has demonstrated some social mobility as compared to the first generation, the relative gap between second generation Ashkenazi and Sephardi groups has not narrowed.

The Israeli population is thoroughly urban. Only 3 percent of Israelis live in rural settlements. Almost 60 percent of the population is concentrated in the coastal area between Haifa and Ashdod. Although the overall population density, including the Negev Desert, is 195.5 per sq km, in 1981 Tel Aviv and Haifa had a much higher density at 5,906 and 1,436 persons per sq km respectively.

6. RELIGION. Out of the total population of Israel, 83.2 percent is Jewish and the remaining 16.7 percent is Arab, split among Muslims (80 percent), Christians (12 percent) and Druze (8 percent). The organizational structure of religion in Israel originated during the Ottoman Empire under which religious communities — known as millets — were granted autonomy in religious and personal affairs. Jewish, Muslim, Druze and Christian religious courts have exclusive jurisdiction in personal status matters affecting the respective community members. In matters involving persons of mixed religious communities the President of the Israeli Supreme Court decides which court has jurisdiction.

The Ministry of Religious Affairs was created to deal with the religious communities. It is responsible for nearly 200 religious councils and more than 300 religious committees in towns and smaller communities.

The Jewish millet is officially divided into two separate communities. There is a Supreme Rabbinical Council composed of twelve rabbis but headed by two Chief Rabbis, one each for the Sephardi and Ashkenazi communities. The Chief Rabbinate supervises eight regional rabbinical courts with 65 religious judges (dayanim) and a rabbinical court of appeals headed by the two Chief Rabbis. It is charged with interpreting Jewish law (halacha) which has binding legal and administrative force.

Although less than one-third of the Jews in Israel consider themselves observers of orthodox religious practice, decisions of the Chief Rabbinate are legally binding on the entire Jewish population. Applications of these decisions, notably in matters of personal status, immigration, and citizenship, create tension between religious and secular Jews.

7. POLITICAL STRUCTURE AND LEADERSHIP. Israel has a parliamentary system of government. In the absence of a constitution, the Transition Law of 1949, Basic Laws, and subsequent legislation provide an institutional framework for the government. Legislative power is vested in a 120-member single chamber parliament, the Knesset. The

Knesset is elected every four years on the basis of proportional representation. Executive power is concentrated in a strong cabinet. All Israeli cabinets have been based on coalitions of varying political composition.

The judicial branch is guaranteed complete independence. It provides for magistrate courts in major cities, four district courts and a ten-member Supreme Court. The Supreme Court sits also as a High Court of Justice in actions brought by citizens seeking redress against governmental actions.

The President of the State is elected by the Knesset for a period of five years and may be re-elected for an additional term. Most of his functions are ceremonial and non-political. The proportional representation system has given rise to an extreme form of multiparty system. On the average, 12 parties are represented in the Knesset, a high number even by the standards of European multiparty politics. This is enhanced by the low electoral threshold level which guarantees a seat for any party that can poll one percent of the nationwide vote.

8. MILITARY STRUCTURE. The Israeli Defense Force was created in 1948 in the midst of the War of Independence out of a number of underground military units, the largest of which was the Hagana. The Defense Service Law of 1949 established the legal basis of the IDF and its structure.

The structure of the IDF was closely patterned on the citizen army of Switzerland and has two distinctive components. The Regular Service (Sherut Sadir) is on active duty. Within the Regular Service, the Permanent Service (Sherut Kevah) comprises career commissioned and noncommissioned officers who form the command and administrative structure of the armed forces. The Conscript Service (Sherut Hovah) is made up of men and women who, under the law, are drafted at the age of 18, men to serve for three years, women for 20 to 24 months. National service can be extended during periods of emergency. Exemption from military service is granted to women on grounds of religious conviction or married status and to certain categories of students in yeshivot (theological colleges). Deferment is granted to students who take up designated academic subjects. Except for the Druze and Bedouin, Arab citizens of Israel do not serve in the army.

The Reserve Service (Sherut Miluim) is composed of all able-bodied men under age 49 and able-bodied unmarried women under 39. The reserve system enables Israel to deploy at short notice a large military force while avoiding the necessity to keep a large standing army.

Based on designated military districts, the reserve forma-
tions are issued emergency equipment so that units can be
called up and become operational within a matter of 48
hours. The government does not disclose statistics about
the armed forces, but semiofficial publications estimate
the manpower potential of the IDF at 150,000 in the Regular Service and 300,000 in the Reserve Service.

The IDF has three arms: army, navy, air force. It
is headed by a single General Staff and the Chief-of-Staff
is a Rav Aluf (Lieutenant General) — the only serving
officer of that rank. The General Staff consists of the
Chief of Staff, the chiefs of the Manpower, Logistics, and
Intelligence branches, the Director of Military Training,
the commanders of the Army, Navy, and Air Force, and the
commanding officers of the Northern, Central, and Southern
Commands.

Auxiliary Roles of the IDF. In order to fulfill a
number of paramilitary roles, the IDF established the
Nahal (Pioneering Fighting Youth) which combines military
service with agricultural settlement. Under Labor Party
rule, and again recently, Nahal groups have begun partici-
pating in settlements in the West Bank. Gadna is another
paramilitary organization designed to provide military
training for boys and girls aged 14-18. It is run jointly
with the Ministry of Education.

The IDF has also been in charge of the areas under
Israeli control. Following the establishment of Israel,
the IDF set up the Military Administration which
supervised the Arab population within the pre-1967 borders
until 1966. Following the Six Day War, the newly occupied
territories were also placed under military government.

Military Industry. The Ministry of Defense owns and
runs all factories producing military equipment. Because
Israel has been vulnerable to embargos on military equipment, the military industry has produced a variety of
products from spare parts and ammunition to tanks
(Merkava) and aircraft (Kfir). The military industry has
vigorously cultivated export markets. It is believed that
Israel today is the seventh largest exporter of military
hardware in the world. Along with military hardware, the
IDF also exports military expertise to Third World countries in Africa, Asia, and Latin America as well as to
South Africa.

Military Expenditures Israeli defense expenditures
are high in comparison with those of other Western countries. Israel spends 2 to 3 times as much per capita as

Sweden, a country with roughly double the population and a similar reserve system to mobilize forces. In relative terms, Israel is spending over 30 percent of its GNP on defense, while Sweden spends approximately 3 to 4 percent of its GNP on defense. Nearly 70 percent of defense consumption is domestic consumption, while the rest are imported.

9. FOREIGN RELATIONS. Since its establishment, Israeli foreign relations have been extremely complex, both at the regional and international level. It was founded with the approval of the United States and the Soviet Union as well as Western Europe, but with little input from the Third World, which at that time was little represented in the UN. From the beginning, the creation of Israel was opposed by most of the neighboring Arab and Islamic states.

Arab States. Israel has historically had hostile relations with Arab states, stemming from Arab non-recognition, and Israel's refusal to deal with the problem of Palestinian refugees. This enmity has been displayed throughout the entire period in border clashes, incursions, and less frequent major wars. In the 1956 Suez Campaign Israel, France and Great Britain attacked Egypt, and in the 1967 June War, Israel fought Egypt, Jordan, and Syria, acquiring by force 68,588 sq km of territory. In 1973, Egypt and Syria attacked Israel, resulting in the direct involvement of both superpowers, and culminating in the Arab oil boycott. Israel's policy has been to divide the Arab world. It effectuated this policy by removing Egypt, the most powerful of the Arab states, from the group of confrontation states. In 1978, and again in 1982, Israel invaded Lebanon, where the disintegration of the central government had permitted the establishment of Palestinian military installations in southern Lebanon, seen as a threat to northern Israel. Currently, Israel occupies 2,800 sq km of Lebanese territory south of the Awali River.

The West. Starting in the 1950s and up until the 1967 war, Israel which had initially tried to pursue a neutral foreign policy, built up strong ties with the West. During the period, Israel's strongest allies in the West were France for military supplies, Germany and to a lesser extent the United States for economic aid. The initially modest economic contribution of the United States increased after the 1967 war to include large scale military and economic aid. In the 1970s, ties with Western Europe worsened following the 1973 Arab oil boycott and Israeli policy in the occupied territories. After the 1973 war, the United States sponsored a series of negotiations between Israel and Egypt and Israel and Syria which led initially to the disengagement agreements and ultimately to the Camp David accord and peace treaty between Israel and Egypt in 1979. However, strains have developed over the Lebanese invasion and Israeli settlement policy in the West Bank. Despite these strains, the special relationship between Israel and the United States was recently institutionalized in the form of a de facto strategic cooperation.

Soviet Bloc. Initially, Israel enjoyed the support of the Soviet Bloc in both political and military terms. However, due to the pro-Arab shift in Soviet policy and the Israeli refusal to support the Communist side in Korea, the relationship deteriorated. The turning point was the Soviet arms sale to Egypt in 1955. Following the 1967 war, all of the Eastern bloc countries with the exception of Rumania broke diplomatic relations with Israel.

Third World. In the 1960s Israel developed substantial ties to many black African nations and states in Latin America. These ties were gradually loosened following the 1967 war, culminating in a massive rupture in diplomatic relations after the 1973 war, in part due to the promise of massive Arab aid. In recent months, there had been some very minor repair of relations with black Africa, with the restoration of consular relations and increased trade. Throughout the period, Israel has nurtured its relations with South Africa, Taiwan, and Latin America, especially in the realm of arms trade and military expertise.

10. ECONOMIC STRUCTURE. The structure of the economy is diversified and includes a mixture of governmental, cooperative, and private enterprises. The large imports of capital derived from public and semipublic sources in Israel and abroad passes through governmental channels and results in the enlargement of the public and semipublic enterprise sector such as Histadrut (the General Federation of Labor). Under the Likud, government policy has been increasingly directed towards encouraging private enterprise and limiting the public sector.

In spite of overall impressive progress, economic growth has proceeded at an unsteady pace. In the 1949-72 period, the annual rise in GNP grew by an average 10 percent in real terms, with the exception of the 1966-67 period when it slowed down because of a policy of economic consolidation. During 1972-82, the GNP annual growth decreased; in 1981 the GNP grew only by 5 percent. Both in 1982 and 1983 the GNP registered zero growth.

BOP and Inflation. One of the most serious problems in the economy is the balance of payment. Israel's foreign trade has consistently shown an extremely adverse balance, owing to the rise in population, the steady increase in consumption especially of imported goods, the expansion of the economy which required heavy imports of machinery and raw materials, and the ever increasing imports of military hardware. The foreign debt rose from less than $300 million in 1952 to over $23 billion in 1983. This amounts to about $5,000 per capita, making Israel the most indebted country in the world.

Another acute problem faced by the Israeli economy is the inflationary pressure created by the disparity between the money supply and the growth of real resources at constant prices. The rapid rise in money supply has been due to three factors operating in varying degrees at different times: credit extended to the government (that is, deficit financing of the state budget), expansion of credit to the public, and monetarization of surplus balances of foreign currency (such as German reparations). In recent years there has been an increasing tendency to resort to deficit financing of the budget. The annual inflation rate has increased steadily from 31.4 percent in 1976 to 194 percent in 1983.

Because of their efforts to encourage immigration and decrease emigration, Israeli governments have been committed to a policy of full employment. With the brief exception of the early 1950s and the recession of 1965-67, when unemployment reached about 10 percent, the unemployment rate has oscillated between 3 and 5 percent. Recent governments have been particularly reluctant to undertake the unpopular policies of cutting down the level of consumption and restraining the increase in the level of consumption. Moreover, the level of private consumption has been growing faster than the GNP; in 1982, there was a net 5 percent increase in private consumption despite the zero growth of the GNP.

As a result, one of the most striking features of the Israeli economy is the almost complete absence of the usual business cycles. The only recession took place in 1965-67, spurred by governmental action to curb inflation and restore the balance of payment. This was abruptly terminated by the 1967 war.

Agriculture. The total cultivated area has been expanding steadily, reaching 4 million dunum in 1980 (1 dunam = approximately 0.25 acre). The main problem has been shortage of water. Despite irrigation programs, Israel has reached the limit of the potential water resources. In the 1970s, sophisticated methods were developed to compensate for the lack of water resources, including cloud seeding, reducing evaporation, and intensifying yields from land already irrigated. High yield nursery-grown vegetables and flowers were introduced, which together with citrus crops constitute 15 percent of Israel's exports. Israel is about 90 percent self-sufficient in food production, but has to import beef and fish. The main forms of agricultural settlements are the kibbutz (where all property is jointly owned and land is leased from the Jewish National Fund) and the moshav (a farmers' smallholder cooperative). In the latter, the land leased from the JNF is divided into separate units that are farmed individually by the members. About 3 percent of the Jewish population of Israel lives in agricultural settlements. Agriculture among the Arab population is based on various mixes of private and communal ownership of land.

Industry. Industrial development in Israel has been hampered by lack of natural resources, limited energy resources, lack of competition, and distance from export markets. Industrial production showed only a 2 percent rate of increase through 1981 and 0.6 percent for 1982. The diamond cutting and polishing industry was the first in the world in 1971, and is Israel's most important export product. It has declined since the turn of the decade, but it still accounted for 17 percent of total exports in 1981. The fastest growing industries are electronics and military. Most of the electronic plants are based on sophisticated technology and specialize in electronic equipment for communications and military use. Total industrial export has risen dramatically over the years and accounted for 61.4 percent of exports in 1981. Exports from the military industry have doubled in the past five years, exceeding $1.2 billion in 1982.

Tourism and Shipping. Since the 1967 war, tourism has expanded rapidly and has become one of the major sources of foreign exchange in Israel. The average number of tourists increased 294 percent from 1968 to 1980. However, because of the worldwide recession and the war in

Lebanon, the number of tourists dropped in 1982 to 996,000, a decrease of 12 percent from 1981.

Shipping serves a vital function in the economy and in communication with other countries as a result of the closed land frontiers with Arab countries. Israel's access routes to both the Atlantic and Indian oceans have stimulated the growth of its merchant fleet, which numbers more than 100 ships. The major shipping company is Zim.

Financial Services. There are more than 40 commercial banks and mortgage and investment banks in Israel. Financial services are dominated by the three big commercial banks: Bank Leumi, Bank Hapoalim, and Bank Discount. The commercial banks wield more power and influence than their counterparts in other countries because of their large investments in all sectors of the economy, their role in channeling the massive subsidized loans of the government to agriculture and industry, and their leading role as both major share holders and brokers in the Stock Exchange. The banks and other financial institutions are supervised by the Bank of Israel, which issues currency, acts as the sole fiscal and banking agent for the government, and regulates the supply of money.

11. INFRASTRUCTURE. Israel is heavily dependent on imported oil to meet its energy needs. The oil fields in the Sinai were given up in 1979 only after American and Egyptian assurances of continued supplies. Moves have been made to switch to power generation by coal, purchased abroad as well as solar energy. Total electric capacity in 1981 was 3,032 mw. The government has also proposed the construction of a canal which would use the altitude difference between the Mediterranean and the Dead Seas to generate hydroelectricity. The canal is controversial both because it would pass through the occupied Gaza Strip, and because of potential damage to Jordanian industry on the other shore of the Dead Sea.

Israel is also facing a serious shortfall in water within the next ten years. The per capita consumption of water is four to five times higher than that of other states in the Middle East, approaching the level of Europe. Four-fifths of this water is used for irrigation in agriculture. The country presently consumes 95 percent of its annual water budget. There is particular concern that overpumping of the groundwater in the coastal plains is leading to gradual encroachment of seawater. Israel

shares an important aquifer with the West Bank, and currently 40 percent of Israeli water originates outside the
pre-1967 borders.

Communications. There are four radio programs offered
by the Israel Broadcasting Authority. Three are geared to
the domestic public (two carry commercial advertising),
and the fourth broadcasts overseas in ten languages under
the name of The Voice of Israel (Kol Israel). Television
is transmitted on one channel; efforts to introduce additional channels have not succeeded because of coalition
politics. Israeli viewers in some parts of the country
are able to receive television transmissions from Jordan,
Lebanon, Syria, and even Cyprus; Jordanian television
offers a special Hebrew-language edition of the news.

The press is highly developed in Israel, with 27
daily newspapers (14 Hebrew, 4 Arabic, and 9 others), and
23 weeklies and fortnightlies. The most prestigious daily
newspaper is Ha'aretz, but it has a limited daily circula-
tion of 50,000 (about 15 percent of the public reads it).
The two most popular papers are the evening Ma'ariv and
its competitor Yediot Aharonot, which are read by about 70
percent of Israelis. While Ha'aretz is politically
neutral and is critical of present government policy, both
Ma'ariv and Yediot lean to the political right. Other
dailies cater to specific audiences, some are owned by
political parties, such as Labor's Davar and Mapam's al-
Hamishmar. Others are printed in foreign languages, the
most respected being the English-language Jerusalem Post.

The Israeli telephone system has been inadequate to
serve the growing population. There were 1,302,000 telephone lines in 1982. However, only two thirds of Israeli
families have telephones and demand for installation far
exceeds supply. Waiting periods for service in heavy
demand areas can reach 5-7 years. The number of requests
for telephone installation was 202,000 in 1982. The
quality of reception is poor and there are frequent break-
downs. Efforts to improve the telephone service by
turning it into a public company have been strongly
resisted by the employees of the Ministry of Communication.

Israel's international communication is served by a
fully automated telephone system, cable and telex. The
telex is the most basic communication service and is
dispensed through 14 telex stations. In 1982 there were
4,100 telex lines including two modern electronic telex
stations in Tel-Aviv and Haifa.

Transportation. There are over 11,950 km of paved roads in Israel, which in 1981 carried a total of 592,906 vehicles, of which 76.5 percent were private cars, 16.2 percent trucks and trailers, 4.5 percent motorcycles, with the remaining 2.8 percent split among taxicabs, buses and other vehicles. There are 500 km of railroads, which in 1980 carried 2,906,000 passengers and 5,025,000 metric tons of freight. El Al, the national air carrier, which had been plagued by mounting deficits and troubled industrial relations, was closed down by the government in 1982. It resumed operations in January 1983 under new management.

12. SOCIAL SERVICES. Education is compulsory and free for all children between the ages of 5 and 16. It is financed partly by the state and partly by the local education authorities. Four types of schools exist: public secular schools, public religious schools, the independent religious schools of Agudat Israel, and public schools for Arabs. There are also a handful of private schools and the separate network run by the Kubbutzim. In 1982-83 the educational system enrolled 1,306,651 students, of which 1,105,730 were in the three branches of the Hebrew education systems, and 200,921 were in the Arabic system. In addition, there are seven institutions of higher learning with a total enrollment of 62,365. There are also about 300 Yeshivot (Talmudic colleges) mostly in Jerusalem. The number of Yeshivot and Yeshiva students has increased dramatically in the past decade; in 1976 there were 28,000 students compated to 54,000 in 1984.

The literacy rate in Israel is about 90 percent among the Jewish population; the number of college graduates per thousand population is the third highest in the world, after the USA and USSR. There are pockets of functional illiteracy, especially among Sephardic Jews, estimated at 300,000 adults. About 11 percent of those over age 14 have had less than five years of schooling, while nearly 30 percent have had more than 13 years of education. The expenditure on education, culture, and entertainment was estimated at 10.3 percent of total consumption expenditure in 1983.

One important institution for social services is the Histadrut which provides welfare services including the most popular medical plan, Kupat Holim, in which about half of the population of Israel participates. The number of hospitals in 1983 was 145, and there were 27,000 hospital beds.

II. POLITICAL ANALYSIS

1.
SUMMARY AND CONCLUSIONS

1.1 POLITICAL EVOLUTIONS. The results of the July 1984 Parliamentary elections in Israel confirmed the durability of a fundamental partisan realignment which started seven years ago. This realignment began in 1977 when the rightist Likud party ousted Labor from power for the first time in the country's history. Although neither major party won enough Knesset seats in the 1984 elections to form a government, Likud's strong showing (41 seats to Labor's 44 out of a total of 120) demonstrated that it had won a loyal following among the Israeli electorate. Despite the handicaps of the retirement of its charismatic leader, Menachem Begin, an unprecedented economic crisis, and an unpopular war in Lebanon, the Likud was able to achieve near parity with Labor. Likud's achievement also came at a time when the Labor Party was united to an unusual degree and presented voters with a clear choice on many issues. The transformation in Israeli politics is evident when the Likud's electoral fortunes in 1977, 1981, and 1984 are compared to those of its predecessor, the Herut party. Until its 1977 victory, Herut was almost universally regarded as an extremist fringe movement.

The 1984 Knesset elections also saw an increase in the strength of parties ideologically to the right of Likud, such as Tehiya and Kach. Ultra-orthodox Jewish religious parties also improved their position vis a vis the established and more moderate National Religious Party.

1.2 FUNDAMENTAL CLEAVAGES. Party politics in Israel reflect several fundamental cleavages that pervade the society. In addition to the Sephardi-Ashkenazi division, ethnicity separates Jews and Israeli Arabs (i.e. Arab citizens of Israel). Israeli Arabs currently make up 15% of the population and are expected to comprise 20% by the end of the century. Increasing political sophistication among Israeli Arabs as well as their growing demographic strength, is likely to result in more insistent demands to broaden the now limited scope of their political power and economic opportunities.

A collective ownership-free enterprise cleavage separates those who support state ownership and control of the economy and those who advocate principles of free enterprise.

A religious-secular split pits those who want the Jewish state to be governed by the laws of the Torah against those who are committe to a large degree of separation between church and state.

Finally, there is a maximalist-minimalist differentiation over the question of what territories Israel should retain permanently. This is likely to be the most divisive of the major cleavages in Israeli society. Support for the maximalist position which calls for retention of the Golan Heights, all of the west Bank and Gaza, has grown steadily since 1967. The Likud and the smaller parties that advocate the maximalist position together won 57 seats in the 1984 elections. When the right wing of the Labor party is taken into account, the maximalists appear to be a slender majority.

1.3 PROSPECTS FOR THE NATIONAL UNITY GOVERNMENT. The present National Unity government, owing to differences that place Labor and Likud at opposite sides of most of Israel's cleavage lines, is unlikely to be able to take decisive action on any policy issue of major importance. Future Israeli politicics will focus on competition for the growing Sephardi and youth vote. Since both parties show marked conservative, nationalistic tendencies, the rightward trend is likely to continue unless new outside influences affect the domestic political environment. The Labor Party is likely to try to recoup its standing and appeal to the electorate in the future by minimizing its differeces with the Likud.

1.4 THE ECONOMY. By ordinary statistical standards, the Israeli economy is deeply troubled. The 1984 projected rate of inflation, for example, is 400-600 percent. Foreign debt totaled over $20 billion, or $45,350 per capita at the end of 1983 (the highest per capita debt in the world). The GNP has recorded no growth in the last two years. These conditions are the result of a combination of policies the most important of which are: full employment, comprehensive welfare, heavy defense spending (now about one-third of the budget and a quarter of GNP), subsidized commodities, and consumer imports. Although

Israel is undoubtedly facing an economic crisis, these statistics conceal unique circumstances that ameliorate the effects usually associated with such negative indicators.

The impact of inflation is greatly reduced by widespread indexing. Most salaries and savings interest rates, for example, have been fully linked to the consumer price index. The unusual structure of Israel's foreign debt also cushions the economic impact that the total figure above would imply. Only 13 percent of the debt is in short-term loans, making immediate default unlikely. Less than 25 percent comes from commercial sources. The remainder is owed to the U.S. government (which recently has shown a tendency to convert loans to grants) and to holders of Israel Government Bonds.

Israel's economic policy has passed through several distinct phases in recent years. In 1977 the LIkud inherited a semi-socialist, service-dominated economy and a 31 percent annual inflation rate from the years of Labor rule. The Likud pledged to reduce governmental involvement in the economy, abolish foreign currency regulators, limit deficit spending and increase exports while curtailing imports. In office it acted only to liberalize foreign currency regulations and offer limited incentives to private business. By 1979 public consumption, the trade and budget deficits and external debt had all increased. Inflation had reached 78 percent. A new finance minister, Yigel Hurwitz, was then appointed to institute an austerity program. But by June 1980, Cabinet resistance to budget and subsidy cuts and the approach of elections led to Hurwitz's replacement by Yoram Aridor, who oversaw what has been called the "election economy." Efforts to stimulate private consumption, including imports, and expand government spending contributed to Likud's 1981 election victory but also led to Israel's current triple-digit inflation, a problem further exacerbated by the 1982 invasion of Lebanon. A stock price collapse, early in the year and a banking shares drop in September 1983 left public conficence in the economy badly shaken. Yigal Cohen-Orgad then took over as finance minister and instituted austerity measures that resulted in an 8.5 percent decrease in real wages but no drop in inflation. The Labor-Likud National Unity Government instituted a temporary wage and price freeze shortly after taking office and has appealed for large-scale increases in aid from the USA and world Jewry. The coalition government is not likely to be able to effect major economic reforms. It will take additional austerity measures, perhaps even risking major labor unrest, but it will rely primarily on increased foreign aid to sustain the Israeli economy in the short- and middle- term.

1.5 LEBANON. Israel's occupation of South Lebanon continues to be the most divisive issue in Israeli politics. The war and occupation have so far claimed the lives of more than 600 Israeli soldiers and have cost more than $1 billion. Approximately 24,000 Israeli troops remain in Lebanon at a cost of nearly $500,000 per day. Domestic opposition, unprecedented for an Israeli military operation, has attended the Lebanon action from the beginning. At least 134 soldiers have been prosecuted for refusing to serve in Lebanon. An early and complete Israeli withdrawal is unlikely, however. While Israel has largely achieved its objective of eradicating the PLO's territorial base in Lebanon, and apparently abandoned its objective of bringing Lebanon into its sphere of influence, the National Unity Government is not agreed on conditions for withdrawal. Likud and some Labor cabinet ministers continue to stress the need for the Israeli-supported "South Lebanese Army" to police part of South Lebanon after an Israeli withdrawal. Lebanon and Syria are not likely to accept this, nor is the SLA itself likely to prove capable of policing the south for some time. Partial Israeli withdrawals, aimed primarily at reducing casualities and placating domestic opinion, may take place in 1985.

1.6 THE OCCUPIED TERRITORIES AND THE PALESTINIANS. Approximately half of the Israeli public is currently committed to permanent retention of the West Bank and the Gaza Strip. Most of the remaining half is prepared to return between 50 and 70 percent of these territories to Arab rule. Only a small portion favors near total Israeli withdrawal. Public commitment to keep the Golan Heights, formally annexed in 1982 according to Israeli law, is somewhat stronger.

The present National Unity Government has agreed to maintain and expand the network of Israeli settlements in all of these territories. Serious consideration of any territorial concessions to any Arab negotiating partner would bring about the fall of the National Unity Government and necessitate new elections.

Although irredentist sentiment and the Israeli settlement infrastructure have grown steadily over the last seventeen years, Palestinian and other Arab opposition to Israeli control of these territories has not diminished.

The high Palestinian birth rate and a recent reduction in emigration from the West Bank and Gaza reinforce the Arab demographic hold on the territories. Recently, terror attacks by groups of Jewish settlers against Palestinians have challenged the Israeli government's ability to maintain law and order in their territories. The attacks continue despite the arrest and prosecution of many alleged Jewish terrorists in 1984.

The present government, prompted by the USA, plans to improve the "quality of life" for Palestinians in the West Bank and Gaza, but this will not extend to the freedom to conduct political activity. At the same time, Likud ministers oppose some of the proposed economic measures to benefit Palestinians, leaving the future of the "quality of life" plan in doubt. Continued political stalemate on the Palestinian issue and an overall deterioration of the situation in the occupied territories are probable unless international factors change the local political balance.

1.7 RELATIONS WITH EGYPT AND PROSPECTS FOR OTHER PEACE NEGOTIATIONS. Since recalling its ambassador from Tel Aviv in response to Israel's 1982 invasion of Lebanon, Egypt has linked an expansion of Israeli-Egyptian relations to improvement in the wider Israel-Arab arena. Progress toward an Israeli withdrawal from Lebanon or an improvement in West Bank conditions would quickly prompt Cairo to return its ambassador. Any further thaw would depend upon additional positive developments in Lebanon or the Palestinian issue and resolution of the Egyptian-Israeli dispute over their border at Taba, south of Eilat along the Sinai coast.

New attempts at wider negotiations are likely, if only to avoid the impression of stalemate. Egypt, Jordon and Palestinians, backed by Saudi Arabia and Iraq, might undertake an initiative looking for at least an American if not an Israeli response. Given public opinion and coalition politics in Israel, any Israeli response is likely to be limited, pending a new government or new elections.

1.8 THE U.S.-ISRAEL "SPECIAL RELATIONSHIP." Closer Israeli-American political-strategic collaboration and steadily increasing American aid distinguished the relations of the first Reagan Administration and the previous Likud Government. These trends will continue. U.S. aid is likely to double, an increase comparable to that which followed the 1973 war. The likelihood that aid levels will be conditional on Israeli policies is remote. The Reagan Administration has minimized the significance of Israeli-American differences in this field and Israel has assumed a more important place in U.S. global strategic planning.

1.9 OTHER FOREIGN RELATIONS. Israeli relations with western Europe have recently shown significant improvement after reaching a nadir at the time of the European Community's 1980 Venice Declaration. New approaches to Black Africa have also borne some fruit. Israel's growing role as a supplier of arms and military advisors to some Third World countries is perhaps the most important development of recent years. Recipients include Guatemala, Honduras, El Salvador, the Nicaraguan contras, and Sri Lanka. Israel has also supplied Iran with spare parts and cooperates with South Africa on military research.

2.
POLITICAL STRUCTURE

2.1 POLITICAL INSTITUTIONS. Israel has a parliamentary system of government. In the absence of a constitution, the Transition Law of 1949, the Basic Laws and regular laws provide the constitutional framework for the government within the context of parliamentary sovereignty.

The legislative power is vested in a 120-member single-chamber parliament, the Knesset. The Knesset is elected every four years on the basis of proportional representation. The last election was held in July 1984.

Executive power is vested in a strong cabinet. The Basic Law of 1968 provides for a cabinet composed of a Prime Minister and an unspecified number of ministers. Since no Israeli party has ever achieved a parliamentary majority, all Israeli cabinets have been based on coalitions of varying political composition. Until 1977, Labor (Mapai) led a center-left-religious coalition which included the moderate National Religious Party. After 1977 Likud gained power with a center-right-religious-ultra-orthodox coalition. In the 1984 elections neither Labor nor Likud achieved a large enough majority to lead a coalition. As a result the two parties formed a National Unity cabinet.

The judicial branch is guaranteed complete independence. It consists of magistrate courts in major cities, four district courts and a ten-member Supreme Court. The Supreme Court sits also as a High Court of Justice in actions brought by citizens seeking redress against governmental actions. Since the victory of Likud, the High court of Justice has increasingly had to deal with a variety of politically sensitive issues, including the expropriation of Arab land in the occupied territories.

A network of religious courts serves the religious communities. Each of the communities in Israel – Jewish, Muslim, Druze, and Christian – has its own religious courts which rule on matters of personal status, marriage, divorce, or alimony. Religious rulings can be appealed in civilian courts.

The military courts have jurisdiction over all military personnel (regular and reserve) and security-related offenses. The military courts play a particularly prominent role in maintaining law and order in the occupied territories. The legal structure of the IDF also includes the post of Advocate General, who acts as chief prosecutor for the military.

The Civil Service is headed by a Commissioner who is appointed by the cabinet. The method of appointment is regulated by law which also restricts political activities of civil servants. The State Comptroller is charged with overseeing the legality, efficiency, and ethical integration of the public service.

The President of the State is elected by the Knesset for a period of five years and may be re-elected for an additional term. Most of his functions are ceremonial and non-political.

2.2 ETHNIC STRUCTURE. The ethnic structure in Israel is highly heterogeneous. Among the Jewish population, there is a major division between the Ashkenazim, from East and Central Europe and America, and the Sephardim (Oriental) Jews, who come mostly from Arab countries, Asia and Africa. A minority of 17 percent in 1940, the Sephardim now make up about 55 percent of the Jewish population and half of the electorate.

Ethnic cleavage has become a cornerstone of social stratification in Israel. In terms of social status, there are major differences according to ethnic origin. While the second-generation (native-born) Sephardim have demonstrated some social mobility, the relative gap between the second generation of the two ethnic groups has not narrowed. In terms of per capita income, only 14 percent of the top 20 percent are Sephardi; in the lowest 20 percent of the income bracket, 60 percent are Sephardi.

Ethnic cleavage is even more pronounced with regard to Jews and Arabs. Although the Arabs occupy the lowest rank in social stratification, they have made significant progress since the early days of the state. The Ashkenazi-Sephardi and the Jewish-Arab divisions which underlie the socioeconomic cleavage generate considerable political tension. Because of the high rate of inter-ethnic marriage (25 percent) among the Jews, Ashkenazi-Sephardi differences are expected to level off in the future, but the tension between the growing Arab minority and the Jews will most likely increase.

Occupational Employment
by Ethnic Group Among Israeli Jews
(in percent)

Sector	Immigrants		Israeli-Born	
	Ashk.	Seph.	Ashk.	Seph.
Scientific, academic, professional, managerial	32.4	11.8	42.0	12.5
Clerks, commerce, services	36.7	41.2	33.3	41.0
Agriculture	5.2	4.7	7.1	4.0
Industry, Transport	25.5	42.1	17.4	42.4

Occupational Employment by Ethnic
Group Among Jews and Arabs in Israel
(in percent)

Sector	Arabs	Jews
Scientific, academic, professional, administrative, managerial	9.0	25.2
Clerks, commerce, services	21.2	38.4
Agriculture	16.2	5.4
Industry, transport	58.1	31.0

2.3 POLITICAL LEADERSHIP. During the tenure of the Labor
Party in government, political leadership was recruited
from three major sources: (1) the "Founding Fathers,"
the socialist Zionist leaders who came to Palestine
between 1904 and 1923 (Ben-Gurion, Sharett, Meir,
Galilee); (2)—the native-born younger generation, with
military background either in the underground Hagana and
Palmach or in the IDF (Allon, Rabin, Dayan); (3)—the Labor
technocrats, (Eban, Peres). The Sephardic population was
underrepresented and appeared as a symbolic "token"
representation (e.g., Hilel, Shitrit). The domestic
political perspective of the Labor elite was liberal-
socialist; in foreign policy it varied from the dovish
(Sharet-Eban) to the hawkish (Meir-Dayan-Rabin).

During Likud's tenure, the sources of leadership
became more heterogeneous. The Likud coalition leaders
derived from: (1) Revisionists and the Irgun and Lehi
underground, predominantly Ashkenazi (Begin, Shamir,
Meridor); (2) technocrats (Gideon Pat, Itzak Mudai, Moshe
Arens, Yuval Ne'eman); (3) the military (Weitzmann,
Sharon, Eitan); (4) Sephardi leaders who have risen
through local politics (David Levy, Meir Shitrit, Moshe
Katzav, Aharon Abuhatzeira); (5) religious leadership,
including rabbinical circles and Gush Emunim (Haim
Drukmann, Hanan Porat).

The domestic perspective of the Likud coalition
leadership varies from a traditional laissez-faire economy
to a welfare-populist outlook. In foreign affairs, it
displays a rather homogenous hawkish perspective.

The most discernible trend in leadership patterns is
the ascendancy of the Sephardi politicians. Responding to
the changing demographic structure of the Jewish population, all the major parties increased the proportion of
Sephardis in the lists of Knesset candidates for the 1984
elections.

2.4 POLITICAL PARTIES. Proportional representation has
given rise to an extreme form of multi-party system. On
the average, twelve parties are represented in the
Knesset, a high number even by the standards of European
multiparty politics. This is a result of the low
threshold level which guarantees a seat for any party that
can poll 1 percent of the national vote.

The proportional representation system enhanced the
tendency of parties to split and regroup, a basic feature
of Israeli political culture. The system has often been
utilized by disgruntled factions and individuals to

improve their position. In some cases they left their parties, only to rejoin at a later date as an official faction in a coalition. The constant splitting and merging introduces a high degree of fractionalization and instability into the system.

Because of the coalition system, small parties and factions which enter a cabinet coalition often enjoy a leverage far in excess of their electoral strength. This is most likely to happen when a small party is a pivot — i.e., crucial to the maintenance of a coalition majority in the Knesset. During the Labor tenure, the National Religious Party was pivotal. In the first Likud period, Agudat Israel became a pivot and was able to extract significant policy concessions in matters of religion. In the second Likud tenure, between 1981 and 1984, the ethnic Tami party established itself as a pivot to press for pro-Sephardi social and welfare legislature. The party's defection over the austerity program of Likud forced Likud to call a new election.

Political Cleavages and the Party System. The present party system in Israel reflects four major political cleavages.

First, the right-left division separates those committed to collective ownership in the economy, government controls in monetary matters, and an extensive welfare system from those who adhere to the principles of a free economy.

Second, religious orthodoxy pits those who are committed to the separation of state and religion against those who want a state based on the laws of the Torah.

Third, ethnic background separates the European Ashkenazi Jews from the Sephardi Jews who originated in the Asian and African Arab countries. The Ashkenazi-Sephardi division partially overlaps social class as the Sephardim tend to be predominantly blue collar workers with limited education. The external Arab-Israeli conflict and the Zionist ideology of internal unity kept the Ashkenazi-Sephardi cleavage latent for some years. The signing of the peace treaty with Egypt and the mobilization style of the Likud Party has accentuated the Ashkenazi-Sephardi division.

Ethnicity also separates Jews from Arabs in Israel. At first, the Israeli Arabs were a small minority that was kept under a tight system of controls. The Arab population has now increased to more than 15 percent of the total. The increase in size of the Arab community together with an increase in political sophistication has resulted in a demand by Israeli Arabs for more equitable political treatment.

Fourth, the national territorial debate has created a minimalist-maximalist axis designated as doves and hawks. Historically, the minimalists have been identified with the moderate territorial demands of the left wing of the Zionist movement, whereas the maximalists follow the traditional Revisionist claim to the whole of Greater Israel. The occupation of the territories in 1967 transformed the national debate into a rift which overshadows all other political divisions.

Based on their relative positions along the cleavage lines, Israeli political parties are conventionally grouped into socialist, liberal, rightist, religious and ethnic camps. Some interesting patterns can be discerned in the 1984 Knesset. The number of left-wing parties has shrunk considerably since the early days of the State. The political center which was embodied by the large General Zionist Party and the smaller Progressive Party is now represented by the three small factions of Retz, Shinui and Yahad. In contrast, there was a major expansion of the right. The Likud, once the small Herut party, expanded to become one of the two major parties. Moreover, it was upstaged on the right by the radical Tehiya-

1984 Knesset

Faction	Knesset seats	Percentage of votes
Labor Alignment	44	34.9
Likud	41	31.9
Tehiya	5	4.0
D.F.P.E.	4	3.4
N.R.P.	4	3.5
Shas	4	3.1
Yahad	3	2.2
Shinui	3	2.6
C.R.M.	3	2.4
Aguda	2	1.7
Morasha	2	1.6
P.L.P.	2	1.8
Tami	1	1.5
Onetz	1	1.2
Kach	1	1.2

Matzad and Ken parties. Another noticeable trend pertains to the fragmentation of the religious camp. In addition to the traditional Agudat Israel and NRP, which lost over the years more than half their electoral strength, there is the new Morasha, a religious-nationalist party and Shas – a Sephardi-Orthodox party. The Sephardi Tami earned one seat in the Knesset following the pattern of other ethnic parties which have not been able to retain a consistent following.

2.5 RELIGIOUS TENSIONS. Although less than one-third of the Jews in Israel consider themselves observers of orthodox religious practice, decisions of the Chief Rabbinate are legally binding on the entire Jewish population. Applications of these decisions, notably in matters of personal status, immigration, and citizenship, create tension between religious and secular Jews.

One of the most persistent conflicts evolves around the definition of who is a Jew. This is important since, under the Law of Return, Jews are granted automatic citizenship. According to the Orthodox definition, a Jew is any person whose mother was Jewish or who was converted to Judaism according to the halacha. This narrow definition excludes conversion to Judaism carried out by Reform or Conservative rabbis; it has created strong opposition among non-Orthodox American Jews. In addition, the term "Jew" is used as a category of le'om (nationality) on the obligatory identity cards. The secularists claim that the civic definition of a Jew should be based on nationality, but Orthodox circles insist that even the civic definition be based on religious criteria. The issue became politicized when the National Religious Party – and more recently the ultra-orthodox Agudat Israel – threatened to withdraw from the Likud coalition if the Law of Return was not revised to include a halachic definition of who is a Jew.

A less publicized but acute conflict involves the status of the Reform and Conservative movements in Israel. Orthodox Judaism enjoys a virtual monopoly; the Chief Rabbinate and the Ministry of Religious Affairs have officially refused to recognize the Reform movement and have an uneasy relationship with Conservative Judaism. Under pressure from American Jews, the freedom of the Reform and conservative movements to establish religious facilities and provide services has been gradually expanded, but their religious jurisdiction is not legally recognized. Amendment of the Law of Return along Orthodox lines could provoke a sharp conflict between the State of Israel and world Jewry, which is largely non-Orthodox.

Another persistent problem focuses on the efforts of the religious parties to promote Orthodoxy in the public domain. Judaism, like Islam, does not permit full separation between religion and state. Since the early days of the state the religious parties have tried to promote legislation to enforce Sabbath and Kashrut observance. Clauses which provide for such enforcement were guaranteed by the Status Quo agreeement reached by the first Labor Government in which the religious parties participated. The ultra-Orthodox Agudat Israel, which joined the Likud coalition in 1977, initiated a new wave of religious legislation. It broadened the domain of Sabbath observance. Limitations on industrial and commercial activity (its most recent demand is a ban on El-Al flights on the Sabbath) have proven costly to the economy. Agudat Israel succeeded in changing the Anatomy and Pathology Law (1953) to prohibit post mortem examinations without written permission of the family, a provision which hampers medical research and criminal investigations. Likewise, the Abortion Law was amended to prevent state aid for abortions on social grounds. The Agudat Israel achieved a relaxation of the regulations under which women can obtain exemption from military service on religious grounds; this constitutes a potentially serious blow to the women's corps of the army.

The growing influence of the religious establishment has long-term implications on Israeli politics and society. Public acceptance of theocratic political elements has been facilitated through coalition politics and through the educational system, which has come to reflect an increasingly religious spirit.

2.6 MILITARY STRATEGIC PROBLEMS. Israel's environment imposes strategic parameters. The concept of no-war no-peace with the Arab states has become an axiom in the doctrine of national security. This axiom was modified but not eliminated after the signing of the peace treaty with Egypt in 1979.

Strategic space and time resources are asymmetrical. Before 1967, Israel had the lowest ratio of territory to borders of any state in the Middle East. The ratio improved after 1967, but the return of Sinai worsened it again. Even more striking is the asymmetry in the population base of Israel and its neighbors.

Under these cirsumstances, Israel faced the necessity of creating a military establishment with the lowest possible cost in manpower and funds — hence the reserve system. The major weakness of the system is the 48-hour period needed for full mobilization in event of surprise attack. Advance intelligence of the enemy's intention is crucial to close the "48-hour gap." Intelligence failures in 1973 led to development of the concept of "active deterrence," i.e., elimination of potential danger spots before they can become a strategic threat to Israel's security. At the same time, the term security interests was broadened to include secondary security threats, i.e., nuclear facilities in Arab countries, terrorist attacks in Israel, and threats to Israel's orderly occupation of the West Bank and Gaza. The bombing of the nuclear reactor in Iraq and the war in Lebanon, which eliminated the PLO infrastructure there, were undertaken within this framework.

A related strategic concern is to preserve qualitative superiority in weapons and manpower. In terms of weapons systems, the IDF has made spectacular progress in local production and in access to the sophisticated weapons market, especially in the United States. However, the Arab states have also made gains in sophisticated Russian or American/Western equipment.

In maintaining the qualitative superiority of manpower, the record is mixed. In the 1950s and 1960s, the qualitative edge in manpower superiority between the Israeli and Arab armies was vastly in Israel's favor. More recently this ratio has declined, especially in the armor and infantry services. According to Martin Van Creveld, a military historian from the Hebrew University, the qualitative ratio between Israeli and Arab soldiers in the 1973 war was 2.5:1; in the war in Lebanon it was 1.5:1. Other indicators of deteriorating quality are low cohesion, low morale, and a high humber of psychiatric casualties.

Among the reasons for the qualitative decline are specialization, a growing emphasis on technology and hardware, and rapid rotation of field commanders. An additional reason with long-term implications is the changing demographic pattern. About 60 percent of the population is now of Sephardi origin, disproportionately skewed towards the lower socio-economic strata. According to reports published by IDF sources, Sephardi recruits tend to score lower on the entrance test than their Ashkenazi counterparts. In the last 18 enrollments of recruits, (there are approximately four enrollments a year), there has been a relatively high percentage of recruits with low scores and low service motivation. Maurice Roumani, a specialist on Sephardi sociology, indicates that among these low-scoring groups, some 80-90 percent are Sephardi, mostly slum dwellers. Since the relative educational gap between Ashkenazi and Sephardi students is expected to decrease only slightly in the next two decades, the manpower quality of the IDF may decline further as the proportion of Sephardi recruits increases.

Intelligence. The military intelligence collected through the Intelligence Branch of the IDF is supplemented by two civilian establishments: the Mossad (Mossad LeBitachon Leumi-Institute for State Security) and General Security Service, also known as Shin Bet (Sherut Bitachon-Kleli). The Mossad, equivalent to the CIA, is charged with collecting information abroad; the Shin Bet is responsible for internal security and counterintelligence within Israel and the occupied territories.

The three intelligence services coordinate their activities through the Intelligence Committee, chaired by the head of the Mossad and including the Director General of the Foreign Office and the Chief of Police. Interagency fighting and communication problems have plagued the cooperation of the three services. Issar Harel, the early head of the Mossad, struggled to establish prerogatives for Mossad. After the failure of Military Intelligence in 1973, the Mossad and Shin Bet gained greater authority. In the decision to move the Phalangists into the camps in Beirut in 1982, the Mossad overruled Yehoshua Sagui, the head of Military Intelligence. Ironically, the Commission of Inquiry (into the Beirut massacre) urged dismissal of Sagui for his failure to urge his views and for associating himself with Phalangist activities once he was overruled by Mossad. As revealed by the Beirut Massacre, the new Unit for National Security set up in the Ministry of Defense did not contribute to better communication among the intelligence community.

Relations Between the IDF and the Government. Relations between the IDF and the government are not well defined by law. The armed forces are subordinate to the government through the Minister of Defense, who serves as commander-in-chief of the armed forces although his office does not expressly carry this title. The Mininster of Defense need not consult the cabinet or procure Knesset endorsement before making major decisions, including the mobilization of reserve brigades. He refers a mobilization order immediately to the Knesset Committee on Foreign Affairs and Security, but in practice it is difficult to reverse such decisions. During the war in Lebanon, Sharon made a number of major decisions without actually informing the cabinet or Prime Minister, which had only the most general form of prior consent. Communication between the Chief-of-Staff, the Minister of Defense, and the cabinet is not well defined and is mostly informal. This dates back to the days when David Ben-Gurion was both Prime Minster and Defense Minister. Ben-Gurion exercised almost exclusive charge over the Chief-of-Staff; but even so the then Chief-of-Staff Moshe Dayan took independent decisions that jeopardized Ben-Gurion's diplomatic moves. The most notable case in point concerns the events leading to the raid on Gaza prior to the Sinai Campaign in 1956. Yitzhak Rabin, the Chief-of-Staff under Prime Minister Levi Eshkol, provoked a major political crisis by expressing military views detrimental to Israeli foreign policy. The close cooperation which recently existed between Chief-of-Staff Eytan and Defense Minister Sharon went against the policy of the Cabinet.

Another ambiguity derives from civilian oversight of senior promotions in the IDF. Formally, promotions are the prerogative of the IDF and are based on merit. In practice, senior positions (at the level of major general) are subject to civilian supervision. This was especially evident during the Ben-Gurion period and was subsequently relaxed. Upon becoming Defense Minister, Sharon re-instituted strict supervision and overruled a number of senior promotions recommended by the Chief-of-Staff.

The appointment of the Chief-of-Staff requires cabinet approval. In theory, it is a non-partisan appointment, but all Israeli Chiefs-of-Staff to date have been members of the ruling party. Thus, Sharon and Ezer Weitzmann had no chance of becoming Chief-of-Staff during the period of Labor governments. Eytan was the first Likud-appointed Chief-of-Staff. The current Chief-of-Staff, Moshe Levy, is considered a non-political appointment.

2.7 FACTORS FOR STABILITY AND INSTABILITY.

The major factor for stability is Israel's structure that provides an orderly process for political change and a relatively organized channel for conflict resolution between classes, religious and ethnic groups. An important feature of this process is the extreme form of proportional representation. This system provides even small groups with the opportunity for parliamentary representation. However, the coalition system often gives smaller parties, especially the religious ones, a political leverage far in excess of their electoral system.

An additional stabilizing factor is the social cohesion derived from shared religious, national and cultural values. Despite deep ethnic divisions and disagreements between orthodox religious and secular elements, the common religious/cultural heritage has prevented major cleavages from becoming disruptive. Perhaps the most important element in this cohesion is the perception of a common enemy, the Arabs. This perception creates a "community of fate" within Jewish society and inhibits manifestations of destabilizing tensions.

A major factor of instability is the coalition behavior of Israeli political parties and factions. The failure of any Israeli cabinet to survive the full constitutional term of four years indicates the low level of cabinet durability. Since 1949 only five cabinets have exceeded a tenure of 25 months, five endured 20-24 months, three lasted 15-19 months, four lasted 10-14 months, three survived between six and nine months, and four fell in less than 6 months. Since electoral strength is almost equally divided between left and right, current coalitions have barely exceeded the required Knesset majority of 61, making them vulnerable to the defection of individuals and small factions.

Another potential factor of instability is the presence of ethnic cleavages in Israeli society. Although the Ashkenazi-Sephardi cleavage has been largely latent, there have been occasional outbreaks of violence starting with the Wadi Salib riots in 1959 and the Black Panther movement in the early 1970s. Recent outbursts have become more frequent and more violent; they include the use of Holocaust symbolism (swastika daubing and use of the slogan "Final solution to the Ashkenazim"), and violence against Peace Now activists and kibbutz members which culminated in the killing of a Peace Now protester in 1983. Ethnic tensions have destabilizing effects on both domestic and foreign policy. Manipulation of ethnic tension, including appeals based on extremist foreign policy, was used by Likud in its election campaign in 1981. The violence generated by these excesses prompted the major parties to sign a "clean campaigning" agreement in the 1984 elections. The 1984 campaign was relatively orderly but future ethnic tension cannot be ruled out.

A more serious ethnic strain is in Arab-Jewish relations. The Arab minority has become progressively disillusioned with the limited scope of political and economic opportunity. The problem of finding employment for the growing educated element of the community is severe. Reflecting a more sophisticated stand, the Arabs in Israel have moved to use political means to achieve community goals, including a resort to parliamentary tactics and the legal system. A minority of the community has become radicalized to the point where acts of civil disobedience and limited terrorist activity have become common among the dense Arab populations of the Little Triangle and Galilee. Jewish reluctance to grant the Arabs a more equitable civic status only exacerbate these tensions.

An additional source of instability is generated by the tenuous relations between the ultra-orthodox camp and the secular authorities. The militancy of the ultra-orthodox elements has been enhanced by a number of factors, including the growing size of the community (due to high fertility rates and immigration from the United States) and the reluctance of the authorities to prosecute offenders. The use of violence has become routine in both internal struggles of the various ultra-orthodox sects and in action against the secular society. The underground organization Keshet, established a few years ago, is devoted to vandalizing pornographic displays and archeaological digs which infringe on ancient burial sites. The ultra-orthodox have employed violent tactics, including stone throwing, to stop car traffic and close down entertainment on the Sabbath.

The ultra-orthodox activity has provoked a secular reaction. A new group, Hemdet (a Hebrew acronym for Freedom of Science, Religion, and Culture), was formed in April 1984 to combat Orthodox coercion. The cleavage may become even more destabilizing if Agudat Israel and other religious parties lose access to power. During the Likud tenure, Agudat Israel managed to pass a number of bills which satisfied the ultra-Orthodox aspiration to introduce the principles of the religious law, the halacha, into the political system. A reversal of this process under a secular Labor coalition could generate a serious ultra-Orthodox backlash.

Perhaps the potentially most destabilizing factor involves the political and organizational consolidation of the nationalist-religious groups dedicated to the retention of the West Bank. Ever since 1967 there has been continuous public debate over the future disposition of the territories. On one hand, the moderate Social Zionist camp has argued against the annexation of the territories on demographic, democratic, and moral grounds and supported "territorial compromise," the idea of returning greater or lesser portions of occupied territory to Arab neighbors. On the other hand, the nationalist-religious camp has come out in favor of retaining the territories because of their religious significance. This demand was bolstered by the activities of the Gush Emunim, which took the lead in setting the territories. The Gush Emunim was even critical of the scope of activity of the Likud governments, which sharply accelerated the settlement drive after 1977.

The existence of a recently discovered Jewish terrorist underground which has acted against Arab targets in the West Bank indicates that elements in the Gush Emunim

are prepared to circumvent the law of the state in obe-
diance to the "higher law" of religious imperatives. Although the mainstream of the Gush and right-wing politicians have dissociated themselves from the more bizarre
activities of the terrorist groups, such as the attempt to
blow up the Temple Mount, there was tacit support of the
action against the West Bank mayors, who represented the
Palestinian National Guidance Committee. Gush spokesmen
made it clear that they would not abide by a decision of
the authorities to give up the territories. Should any
future Israeli government seriously entertain this idea,
the nationalist-religious camp may involve the specter of
a Kulturkampf. Under such circumstances, a democratic
majority decision may be difficult to implement without
provoking serious civil strife.

3.
EXTERNAL DEVELOPMENTS

3.1 ARAB-ISRAELI CONFLICT. The traditional Labor Party policy toward the Arab-Israeli conflict was based on two interlocking premises: pursuing peace with the Arabs while safeguarding the security of Israel. However, Labor was badly split with regard to the implementation of this policy and never articulated a clear platform. The major point of division was the extent of territorial compromise to be given in exchange for peace. The two official plans, the Allon and Galili plans, showed discrepancies. Internal debates revealed a range of views, from the dovish stand that would have handed over most of the West Bank and Sinai to a more hawkish position which opposed any major territorial concession. A corollary of this division was the lack of clarity regarding Jewish settlement of occupied territories; Labor approved settlements at Yamit in Sinai (the Rafah salient), and at Gush Etzion and the Jordan Valley in the West Bank, but had no clear policy with regard to settlements elsewhere in the West Bank. Regarding the future of the West Bank, there was more consensus. The Labor Party favored the Jordanian option, a federation between Jordan and a Palestinian entity on the West Bank and Gaza. In matters of security, Labor was committed to cautious deterrence, a basically defensive posture with limited preemptive strikes to deal with PLO attacks.

Likud's foreign policy is also based on the premises of peace with security, but there are major differences. Likud's willingness to exchange territory for peace was limited to the Sinai and Egypt. The Golan Heights were officially annexed in 1982, and the West Bank is perceived as part of Eretz Israel (the land of Israel). The Palestinians are offered a limited autonomy, possibly in cooperation with Jordan, but Likud has emphatically rejected negotiation with the PLO. The policy of military deterence has been expanded to include pre-emptive strikes against a wide range of targets, such as countries harboring PLO fighters, and nuclear and military facilities in Arab countries.

3.2 LEBANON. Lebanon became a major concern for Israeli foreign policy following the civil war in 1975. The outcome of this war led to the curtailment of Christian power, the permanent military presence of Syria, and a territorial base for the PLO which it utilized to launch attacks on Galilee. Labor governments tried to contain this situation by enhancing the power of Major Saad Haddad in Southern Lebanon, and by conducting retaliatory actions against PLO strongholds inside Lebanon. Likud continued this policy, but enlarged the scope of the strikes; in 1978 it conducted a major "mopping up" action known as the Litani Operation. These strikes eventually brought about a de facto truce between the PLO and Israel, which was negotiated by the American envoy Philip Habib in 1981.

In June 1982, following an attempt by non-PLO Palestinians to assassinate the Israeli ambassador in London and a subsequent two-day artillery exchange between the IDF and the PLO, Israel invaded Lebanon. The major force behind this decision was Defense Minister Ariel Sharon, who overcame the initial resistance of the government. There were two major assumptions underlying the Israeli move. First, that the political power of the PLO and its influence on the West Bank could be eradicated if its territorial bases in Lebanon were destroyed. As a result, the Palestinians were expected to be more receptive to the de facto annexation of the West Bank. Second, that Israel's active intervention would help the Maronite Phalangists preserve hegemony over the more numerous Lebanese Muslim population. Such a Phalangist government, dependent on Israel for its continued existence, was expected to sign a peace treaty with Israel.

The outcome of the war fell short of most of these expectations. Only the departure of the PLO, which was encircled in Beirut, and the subsequent disintegration of the organization were perceived as a success. The turmoil following the assassination of Lebanese President-elect Bashir Gemayel in September 1982 demonstrated that opposition to the Phalangists was still potent. The ensuing massacre in the refugee camps in Beirut provoked an international outcry that led to the removal of Sharon from his Defense Ministry post. The May 1983 peace agreement, which was negotiated between Lebanon and Israel under U.S. mediation, was never implemented primarily due to Syrian objections. The accord was subsequently abrogated.

3.3 PEACE PROCESS WITH EGYPT. Likud's acceptance of Sadat's peace initiative was based on the long-standing

Israeli assumption that Egypt is the key actor in the Arab-Israeli conflict. Without Egypt, the combination of Arab states would be too weak to mount a credible military offensive. It was also assumed that Egypt's defection would weaken and divide the Arab world as well as deprive the Palestinians of their main advocate. Such a configuration would leave Israel in a more favorable position to pursue its designs in the West Bank. The peace treaty between Israel and Egypt was signed and implemented after Israel's withdrawal from Sinai in 1982.

3.4 RELATIONS WITH OTHER MIDDLE EASTERN STATES. Both Labor and Likud have over the years made contact with a number of moderate Arab states, most notably Jordan, Morocco, and Tunisia. Most of the contacts with Jordan involved disputes over water sharing in the Jordan River system. Morocco was influential in negotiating the initial stages of Sadat's peace initiative. Following the peace agreement with Egypt, there was a brief tendency in the Israeli government to seek a Tel Aviv-Cairo-Riyadh axis. According to persistent but unconfirmed reports, the main architect of this policy was Ezer Weitzmann, then Defense Minister in the Likud cabinet. He was overruled by Begin and Sharon.

Israel has consistently viewed radical Arab states as highly detrimental to its security. Under the Likud government, it has extended the policy of deterrence to include pre-emptive actions against Arab states (e.g., the bombing of the nuclear facility in Iraq). Some tactical arrangements were reached with Syria in Lebanon, but the annexation of the Golan Heights in 1981 virtually precluded any possibility of rapprochement with Syria.

Israel enjoyed a close relationship with Pahlavi Iran, which included economic ties and extensive military cooperation. These ties were severed by the Khomeini Revolution in 1979, but there is evidence that some cooperation in particular providing military spare parts and other arms shipments has been re-established since the outbreak of the Iran-Iraq war. Israel's relationship with Turkey, although low-key, has been traditionally cordial.

3.5 OTHER POLITICAL AND RELIGIOUS ENTITIES. Israel has traditionally aided non-Arab political minorities in the Middle East. Its links to the Maronites in Lebanon go back to the early days of the state. The Kurds in Iraq received Israeli aid until the Kurdish rebellion was terminated in the late 1970s. Israel has also been reputed to have intelligence connections with the Coptic minority in Egypt.

The attitude towards the Palestinians, the largest stateless group in the Middle East, has been shaped by the historical rivalry over Palestine. In the pre-1948 period, the leaders of the Jewish Yeshuv in Palestine had limited contacts with the local Palestinian elite, which were disrupted by competing national aspirations and periodic civil strife. After the foundation of the state, these limited relations were severed. After the 1967 war, which established Israeli rule over more than one million Palestinians, the contacts with the local elite, especially the mayors and notables, were re-established. However, both the Labor and Likud governments have strenuously opposed any links with the PLO. Since most Palestinians living under Israeli rule came to support the PLO, and many leaders and notables were dismissed from office or deported by occupation authorities, the renewal of contacts after 1967 did not lead to any fruitful political dialogue. Nonetheless, the anti-PLO policy is almost unanimously accepted by the Israeli public; only a small number of left-wing politicians have supported negotiations with the PLO.

Outside the region, Israel has a special relationship with the world Jewish community. Unlike other immigrant states, Israel has formally acknowledged this special tie. The Law of Return gives any Jew the right to settle in Israel. The state of Israel has routinely relied on the Jewish community for financial and political help. Despite some disagreements, Diaspora Jewry has largely acknowledged Israel's dominant position as the Jewish state.

3.6 THE UNITED STATES. In the early years following independence, Israel tried to pursue a neutral course in foreign policy and establish friendly but guarded relations with the United States. Increasingly, however, Israel's position has become more pro-western and U.S.-oriented.

Beginning in the 1960s, Israel's relations with the United States became more significant. The United States has provided economic and military aid, has supported Israel diplomatically and has assumed a central position in mediating the Arab-Israeli dispute. This centrality has been enhanced by Israel's growing isolation from its traditional West European allies. While in opposition, Likud traditionally supported a strong pro-American stance; after assuming control of the government, Likud has seen the relationship with the United States as pivotal.

Unlike Labor, Likud has striven to present the relationship as near parity. In this view, Israel is an asset, not a liability, to the United States. As "the only stable and democratic regime in a volatile region," Israel is presented as crucial to U.S. interests, providing an outpost against direct communist expansion or indirect efforts to destabilize pro-western regimes. The major proponents of this view have been Begin and Sharon. It was at the latter's initiative that the Agreement of Mutual Understanding between Israel and the United States was signed in 1981.

The equal partnership perspective has been used by Likud to redefine the U.S.-Israeli relationship in military/economic/diplomatic matters and to deal with the divergence of interest over the occupied territories. Unlike Labor, Likud does not assume that the level of U.S. assistance is conditional upon Israel's willingness to follow the American lead. The terms of the Camp David Agreement were seen by Likud as an adequate Israeli concession to American interests in the region. Likud has been encouraged in this approach by the American response, reflecting de facto acceptance of the precept that U.S. aid is not to be used to pressure Israel.

3.7 WEST BLOC COUNTRIES. Israel's relations with western Europe have undergone a number of dramatic changes. The apex of Israeli-West European cooperation came during the Sinai Campaign in 1956, in which Britain and France collaborated with Israel in military operations against Egypt. Following the 1967 War, France and Britain began a process of disassociation from Israel. Other common market members followed suit. This process accelerated after the 1973 War because of Europe's dependence on Arab oil and its growing concern over the Palestinian issue.

Likud's accession to power exacerbated the European-Israeli alienation. Among the most decisive factors were Likud's hard-line approach to the occupied territories and Begin's trenchant political style. On several occasions Begin undiplomatically attacked a number of European heads of state. The nadir in the relationship to date was reached when the European Community adopted the Venice Declaration in 1980 supporting Palestinian claims to sovereignty.

Israel's relations with non-European western bloc countries, such as Japan, Australia, and Canada have been correct but not cordial. Japan's dependence on Arab oil has mandated a rather neutral relationship. Occasional public support for the PLO by Australia and Canada has drawn Israeli rebuffs.

The only exception to this pattern is South Africa. In its first two decades of independence, Israel's links with South Africa were limited to a consular-level relationship and small-scale trade. After Black African countries broke off diplomatic ties with Israel in 1967 and 1973, the two countries moved to upgrade their relationship. The Labor government established full diplomatic relations with Pretoria in 1974 and the South Africans opened their embassy in Israel in 1975. Israel's pariah status at that time permitted a closer economic relationship including large scale military sales in 1976. According to some reports, Israel and South Africa have cooperated in research and development of military and nuclear systems.

3.8 THE SOVIET BLOC. Soviet-Israeli relations were initially extremely cordial. The USSR had played a crucial role in extending immediate recognition to the State of Israel. The Labor leadership of Israel espoused a leftist ideology, and the new state sought to maintain a careful balance of good relations with both superpowers. Relations began to deteriorate in the 1950s, but Communist countries finally broke diplomatic relations with Israel only in the wake of the 1967 War. Despite periodic rumors, the USSR has so far refrained from renewing diplomatic relations with Israel, which could jeopardize the unstable Soviet influence in Arab countries. Unofficial sporadic contacts between the two countries are maintained through the Israeli Rakah Party (communist) and through the Soviet journalist Victor Lewis, who has visited Israel a number of times.

Rumania is the only communist country that has diplomatic relations with Israel. According to some reports, Rumania was instrumental in mediating the initial stages of Sadat's peace initiative and provides Israel with valuable access to Eastern Europe. Unofficially, Israel has developed economic ties with other East European countries, most notably with Hungary. Rumors of plans to restore diplomatic relations between Israel and Poland were aborted following the clampdown on Solidarity.

3.9 THE THIRD WORLD. As a regionally isolated nation, Israel sought to expand its circle of friends in Asia, Africa, and Latin America. Latin American countries have traditionally been among Israel's staunchest allies. Of the 74 countries with which Israel has some form of diplomatic relations, 29 are in South America or the Carribean.   In the 1960s, at the instigation of then Foreign Minister Golda Meir, Israel expanded its diplomatic ties with most of the Black African continent.   These relations came to an abrupt end after 1973.   Israeli ties with Asian countries have been tenuous and limited because of the pro-Arab, non-aligned policies of most of the countries of the Asian continent.

The Likud government has tried to break out of the pattern of diplomatic isolation by enhancing ties with other pariah states such as South Africa and Taiwan and by making fresh approaches to Black African countries.

4.
CURRENT SITUATION: INTERNAL DEVELOPMENTS

4.1 IMPLICATIONS OF THE 1984 ELECTIONS. The inconclusive war in Lebanon, which aggravates the chronic problems of the Israeli economy, steadily eroded the power of the Likud government. The Likud coalition suffered a severe setback when Prime Minister Begin, following several months of incapacitation, resigned in September 1983. Although Yitzhak Shamir succeeded in forming a new Likud cabinet, its precarious parliamentary base made it vulnerable. In April 1984, after the defection of the tiny Tami party, the Knesset decided to call new elections in July.

This election was unanimously considered one of the most crucial in Israel's history. First, it was a major test of the durability of the partisan realignment which started in 1977. Numerous academic surveys and commercial polls have indicated that some 70 percent of Labor support comes from higher status, older Ashkenazim, whereas some 70 percent of Likud voters are lower stratum Sephardim and young Israelis. Since the younger and Sephardi voters constitute a majority in the electorate, Labor is bound to lose support unless it can appeal to these groups.

Observers had disagreed as to whether the Sephardim were permanently alienated from Labor. Initially, the Sephardi support for Likud was interpreted as a "protest vote" against the Labor Alignment. The notion of a "protest vote" implied that the Sephardi vote for Likud was a temporary socioeconomic aberration. Some observers even described it as an anti-establishment vote, which would dissipate after Likud's tenure in office. Other observers pointed out that the political culture of the Sephardim made them particularly susceptible to the populist mobilization style of former Likud leader Menechem Begin. Yet others sought explanation in malodorous economic manipulation, the splintering of Labor between Rabin and Peres factions, and Labor's failure to promote Sephardi politicians in its ranks.

All these circumstances were missing in the 1984 election. The election campaign, from which Begin was absent, was conducted according to the "clean campaign" agreement and was highly orderly. The Labor Alignment appeared more unified than at any time in the last decade. Former President Yitzhak Navon, a prominent Sephardi, was among the Labor elite, and the campaign was especially designed to attract Sephardi votes. Yet in spite of these efforts, the slumping economy and the war in Lebanon, there was no indication that Labor increased its support among the crucial electoral groups. Preliminary surveys and aggregate electoral returns indicate that the Sephardi vote, though fragmented, did not benefit the Labor Party. Moreover, there was a switch to the ultra-right among the Sephardi and the younger electorate. A breakdown of the Army vote — young and 60 percent Oriental — reveals that 50 percent went to Likud and 40 percent to Labor. Kach received 2.5 percent of the Army vote, twice its national average, and there was substantial support for Tehiya. Nationwide, towns and suburbs which have high concentrations of Oriental populations tended to support the Likud and Tehiya. In voting districts where the Likud received more than 40 percent of the vote, Kach received more than its national average of 1.2 percent. Overall, the 1984 election seems to indicate that the Sephardi voters, rather than "protesting" against the Labor, have developed a positive identification with the right-wing belief system in Israel.

Second, the elections were considered a crucial referendum on the future of the West Bank. Labor clarified its commitment to the Allon Plan, under which Israel would retain only the strategic Jordan Rift Valley, Gush Etzion, and Old Jerusalem. According to Rabin, such a modification would leave Israel with 38 percent of the Palestinian population; the rest would be free to form a Jordanian-Palestinian federation.

Likud reiterated its commitment to the territorial integrity of all of Israel's land. Palestinians were offered only limited autonomy. Likud also emphasized the need to expand the settlement drive in the West Bank. Both parties made it clear that the disposition of the territories is the most crucial question in Israel's history and one with implications for generations to come.

The outcome of the election confirmed the observation that the Jewish electorate is almost equally divided on the issue. Out of the 114 Knesset mandates which are held by Jewish parties (6 seats belong to the Arab-dominated parties), 57 seats were captured by parties which oppose territorial concessions. They include Likud, Tehyia,

Morasha, National Religious Party, Shas and Kach. The parties which oppose annexation of the West Bank (Labor Alignment, Shinui, Ruta and Yahed) hold 53 seats. The position of Agudat Israel and Tami, which have 3 seats, cannot be easily determined.

1984 Knesset

Faction	Knesset seats	Percentage of votes
Labor Alignment	44	34.9
Likud	41	31.9
Tehiya	5	4.0
D.F.P.E.	4	3.4
N.R.P.	4	3.5
Shas	4	3.1
Yahad	3	2.2
Shinui	3	2.6
C.R.M.	3	2.4
Aguda	2	1.7
Morasha	2	1.6
P.L.P.	2	1.8
Tami	1	1.5
Ometz	1	1.2
Kach	1	1.2

The deep and even cleavage prevented either of the big parties to form a coalition. Instead, the National Unity Government, which includes Labor, Likud, Shas and the National Religious Party was negotiated. Following the agreement, the 6-seat Mapam left the Alignment. Labor lost another leftist member who defected to Ruta, bringing its number of mandates down to 37.

The Labor leader Shimon Peres will serve as Prime Minister for the first two years, to be followed by Likud leader Yitzhak Shamir. Labor received the defense, interior and education portfolios, while Likud was given the foreign affairs, finance and justice ministries. The economic policy of the National Unity Government calls for an austerity plan.

4.2 THE WAR IN LEBANON. The question of the war in Lebanon is undoubtedly the most serious political problem in Israel. The IDF, caught between rival factions, especially in the Shouf mountains, has suffered 155 casualties since hostilities ended in the summer of 1982. To reduce the number of casualties and improve its strategic position, the Israeli cabinet decided in July 1983 to withdraw the IDF to south of the Awali River.

The redeployment, which was completed in September 1983, has not alleviated the problems of the IDF. The casualty rate remains high, as the predominantly Shiite population is hostile towards the Israelis. In addition, there is increased infiltration of PLO elements and Lebanese from behind the Syrian lines and growing local resistence. So far, the war has resulted in more than 600 Israelis dead and more than 3,000 wounded, numbers which constitute 3.3 percent of the 18,000 soldiers killed and 10.3 percent of the 24,000 wounded since 1948. The casualty rate for the war in Lebanon is nearly comparable to that of the Six-Day War in 1967.

The war has also been financially prohibitive. Cost estimates for the invasion include $650 million in domestic outlays and $350 million for imported weapons and ammunition. Indirect costs, through loss of production and reduction of tourism, were calculated at $425 million. The initial daily cost of keeping the 36,000 troops in Lebanon was put at $1 million per day. More recently, the Defense Ministry estimated the annual cost at $130 million. Coupled with the reduction of the military budget, these costs forced the IDF to eliminate some programs and lay off 1,100 civilian and military personnel. This move will save an estimated IS 14 billion and make possible an increase of between 9-24 percent in salaries. According to Deputy Chief-of-Staff David Ivri, such an increase will make IDF salaries competitive with the civilian market and prevent highly trained technical personnel from leaving.

The deployment in Lebanon introduced severe constraints on the training and reserve system of the IDF. Since the war, IDF units have had to be increasingly trained in urban guerrilla tactics, at the expense of the more traditional skills needed in conventional warfare. In addition, reserve duty, which is normally devoted to training, has been "eaten up" by police duty in Lebanon. Following the war the reserve tour of duty was increased, leaving the IDF with little time margin.

The moral and political implications of the war have badly politicized the IDF. Soldiers Against Silence, There Is A Limit, and a number of other anti-war groups have actively denounced the war and spearheaded a drive of conscientious objection to service in Lebanon. So far, more than 130 reservists have been tried and sentenced for refusing their tour of duty in Lebanon. Numerous officers and soldiers have written to Shamir to protest the war and, on one occasion a whole reserve unit turned up for protest outside the Prime Minister's home. These actions come on top of the highly publicized resignation of a high ranking officer during the war, and the continuous, year-long vigil outside Begin's residence.

The politicization of the IDF has serious implications, since many of the combat and elite units are manned by members of kibbutzim and middle-class Ashkenazim who oppose the war. As a result, there was a decrease in military motivation among kibbutz members. Known as the "small head" syndrome, it was epitomized in a refusal of kibbutz members and others to volunteer for elite units and officer training. According to a recently released report by the psychological service of the IDF, this phenomenon is on the decline now. The IDF also released statistics for the August 1984 draft which show that there was a rise in volunteering for elite units.

4.3 THE PROBLEM OF LAW AND ORDER. The prolonged occupation of the territories has created numerous problems for law and order. The first aim of the Israeli Military Government was to maintain public order and safety; however, efforts to delineate the legal principles have become extremely complicated because of the multiplicity of legal sources. The administered territories are governed according to four legal systems: international law, the legal principles established by the Military Administration (most notably, the Military Advocate in the Military Administrations), Jordanian law (binding on the local Arab population) and Israeli law.

The arrival of Jewish settlers, following the successful attempt of Rabbi Moshe Levinger in 1968 to break the Israeli government ban on Jewish settlements, has vastly complicated the legal situation. There was a lack of clarity regarding the legal status of Jewish settlers and the land expropriation undertaken by the government on their behalf. This situation was further aggravated when, in response to Arab resistance to the settlement drive, the settlers embarked on vigilante activities. Jewish attacks on Arabs went largely unpunished, as opposed to stringent measures against comparable Arab activities. In 1980, the charges that the West Bank had a double legal standard prompted the Attorney General Itzhak Zamir to appoint a special committee headed by his deputy Yehudit Karp. The Report, which documented numerous cases of Jewish abuse of Arabs, mainly by civilians, was not implemented until 1983.

The infringement on law and order, which started in the West Bank, quickly spread to Israel proper. It resulted in a dramatic increase in activity against Arab Muslim, Arab Christian, and even pro-Arab Jewish targets. Responding to a renewed wave of Palestinian activity in 1983-84, several small Jewish terrorist groups emerged. Among them were the Rabbi Kachana Splinter group El-Nakam, the Lifta group, which planned to blow up the Temple Mount, and the Ein-Kerem group which carried out a number of attacks on Arab and Christian targets. A Peace Now activist was killed, and several were wounded at a peace rally in February 1983. Most recently, a 27-member group from Gush Emunim was arrested and charged with the attack on the West Bank mayors in 1982, the killings at the Islamic College in Hebron in 1983, and plans to blow up the Islamic edifices on the Temple Mount. In addition, the authorities investigated the killing of two Arabs who survived the attack on the bus which they hijacked in April 1984.

The widespread deterioration in law and order both within the Green Line and the occupied territories — especially the existence of a Jewish underground — has prompted the authorities to take a number of steps. The Military Government acting together with the Ministry of Justice, the Interior Ministry, and the Police, moved to implement the findings of the Karp Committee. The belated but speedy crackdown on Jewish terrorists is indication of this trend.

However, in trying to introduce a more equitable legal status for Jews and Arabs, the Israeli Government faces two problems. According to a series of opinion polls taken in June 1984, such a policy is not popular with the public. A PORI poll found that 51 percent support heavy penalties for Palestinian offenders in the West Bank and 55.3 percent support fully or partially the statement that "Arabs understand only force." The same poll revealed that although 60 percent were against a Jewish terrorist organization, 42.3 percent felt that the policy of the Military Administration in the occupied territories has been too lenient. A Modin Ezrahi poll revealed that 64.4 percent were against the establishment of a Commission of Inquiry into the killings of the two bus hijackers, and 57.2 percent felt that the report should not have been made public. Only 26.6 percent approved of the Commission and 33.9 percent approved of the publication of its findings.

An even more serious problem stems from the stiff penal code reserved for Arab terrorist activity. Life sentences and long-term prison terms are common. In a recently issued order (No. 1108) the Military Government, bowing to pressures from Jewish settlers, recommended penalties of up to 20 years for stone-throwing attacks. Any effort to apply the same penal standards to Jewish offenders may prove difficult. The arrest of the 27 members of the Jewish terrorist organization in the West Bank will provide a major test. So far, both the accused and sentenced members of the group have enjoyed special privileges in the minimum security Tel Mond prison where they are kept.

4.4 ECONOMY. By most statistical measures, the Israeli economy is deeply troubled. For example, 1984's projected rate of inflation is over 400 percent, the external debt reached more than $20 billion by the end of 1983, and the GNP recorded no growth in the last two years. Since Likud came to power in 1977, the CPI has increased by 25,614 percent.

There are a number of reasons for the present development. When Likud won the 1977 election, it inherited an economic system with major structural problems. The combination of full employment, comprehensive welfare, and heavy defense spending manifested itself in growing budget deficits, inflation and continuous dependence on foreign aid. Likud's economic platform was premised on a free economy. It envisaged a reduction of government involvement, stimulation of free enterprise and halting inflation by limiting deficit spending. It also sought to reduce the balance of payments deficit through increases in exports, curtailment of imports, liberalization of business regulations, and the abolition of foreign currency restrictions.

Likud implemented only two of its policies: liberalization of currency exchange regulations and a limited stimulation of private initiative. Moreover, because of political and security cross-pressures, there has been a steady deterioration in most of the other economic indicators targeted for reform. Public consumption, the unfavorable ratio of export to import, budget deficits, external debt, and inflation have all increased dramatically. The inflation rate, which had been 31.4 percent per annum when Likud assumed power, increased to 78.2 percent by 1979. The number of working days lost through strikes and lockouts tripled.

In 1979, a brief effort was made to reverse this trend when Yigal Hurwitz replaced Simcha Erlich as the Minister of Finance. Hurwitz instituted drastic cuts in the budget, abolished food subsidies, and promoted restriction of the work force (only 32.3 percent of the labor force was engaged in productive labor while 67.7 percent were in service occupations). Hurwitz also tried to introduce budget cuts in the military sector.

This austerity policy encountered unprecedented resistance from other ministries represented in the cabinet, each of which fought to retain or increase its allocation. The policy was also unpopular with the public. In June 1979, Likud's popularity rating was 24.9 percent, Begin's personal rating was 40.6 percent, and dissatisfaction with the economy rated 67.4 percent. In June 1980, after a few months of Hurwitz's austerity economy, public satisfaction with Likud was 21.6 percent, Begin's popularity was down to 24.6 percent, while dissatisfaction with the economy was still at 67.3 percent.

In light of its waning popularity, Likud replaced Hurwitz, and the new Minister of Finance, Yoram Aridor received a mandate to change the economic course. The new policy known as the "right economy" or "election economy," reversed most of the previous Likud goals. It aimed at stimulating private consumption, raising the standard of living, and expanding government spending (especially in West Bank-related items). The new policy virtually abandoned the attempt to control wages and phase out subsidies. The inflationary effects of Aridor's economy were increased by the war in Lebanon. According to the 1984 Report of the Bank of Israel, the war resulted in a 7 percent annual increase of security outlays. Together with the "right economy," they resulted in a 292.7 percent inflation rate by 1983. However, during this period, the seriously ailing economy did not translate into private hardship. On the contrary, the standard of living during these years was on the increase and many actually profited from inflation. Public equanimity about the economic situation derived from a number of factors. Indexing in Israel has been widespread. Nearly everything, including bank accounts and bonds, has been linked to the cost of living. Homeowners have until recently profited from inflation. A majority of apartment purchases were made done so with government assistance at low interest rates not indexed to inflation. The subsequent inflation virtually wiped out the mortgages.

During the "boom years," investment was widespread and highly lucrative. According to estimates, between 550,000 and 700,000 Israelis (some 30-40 percent of the labor force) invested in the stock market. The Tel Aviv Stock Exchange was at the time a highly speculative institution; there was no correspondence between the value of stocks and the real value of the assets they represented, there was a preponderance of banking and financial stocks, and there were allegations that fictitious stocks were issued. The value of stocks increased between a few hundred percent and 550 percent in the peak years of 1980-1983. Stock exchange earnings became a major source of income for many Israelis. Some investors gave up jobs to speculate full time on the stock exchange.

In view of the politically unpopular experiment with Hurwitz's "austerity economy," Finance Minister Aridor had few options available to him to cure economic problems. Huge expenditures in the West Bank and the cost of the war in Lebanon further impeded the process. One policy, adopted in September 1982, called for a controlled monthly devaluation of the shekel in relation to the dollar, limiting price rises to 5 percent a month to slow down inflation. This policy backfired badly; it led to an undervaluation of the dollar and a corresponding increase for import items. Expecting a massive adjustment in the value of the shekel, the public increasingly opted for foreign currency and Patam (local residents' dollar deposits). Some sources put the value of Patam in 1984 at $4 billion.

The other policy aimed at restructuring the stock market to make it less speculative and to channel some of the money into less inflationary savings accounts. Following a number of leaks from the Ministry of Finance, the stock exchange collapsed in the last week of January 1983; 300 shares (more than 50 percent) lost between 5 and 60 percent of their values. An even more serious jolt occurred in September 1983 when the banking shares, which were considered safe because they were artificially supported, were deregulated.

By the beginning of October, public confidence in the financial system was badly shaken. Purchase of foreign currency reached epidemic proportions, forcing the government to devalue the shekel by 23 percent. In a last-ditch attempt to save the economy from collapse, Aridor proposed the "dollarization plan." The plan drew sharp criticism and Aridor was replaced by Yigal Cohen-Orgad.

Cohen-Orgad prepared an austerity plan which included a sharp devaluation of the shekel, pruning $2 billion from the budget and removing price subsidies. These austerity measures met with the approval of the International Monetary Fund and the U.S. Agency for International Development, which previously warned Israel of an imminent insolvency. An initial implementation of the plan led to an 8.5 percent lowering of real wages in 1984, but it did not arrest inflation. The moves triggered widespread industrial unrest and a series of crippling strikes in the public sector and services.

In another reaction which was underscored by the lack of confidence in the government's economic policy, the public turned to the black market in dollars. The black market had flourished under Labor, but the monetary reforms of Likud in 1977 did much to control it. Anticipating drastic measures after the election, the public purchased increasing amounts of black market dollars, at prices up to 30 percent above official value. According to a June 1984 estimate, the public had $700 million stored at home. The continuous economic uncertainty prompted more dollar buying in the summer of 1984. Haaretz reports estimated that between January and June, the public bought $840,000, and that since June an additional $1 billion in Patam and black market dollars has been acquired.

Patam and dollar hoarding are harmful to the economy. The dollar deposits of Patam can be redeemed in a Shekel which is continuously devalued, fueling inflation. The hoarded cash is inactive and thus lowers the overall activity of the system. Turned into Shekels, it would increase demand for consumer goods, something which has been one of the traditional sources of inflationary pressure in Israel's economy.

5.
CURRENT SITUATION: EXTERNAL DEVELOPMENTS

5.1 THE WAR IN LEBANON. Since the appointment of the government of Rashid Karame, Israel's relations with Lebanon have steadily deteriorated. The appointment of Karame reflects both the growing influence of Syria and the political-demographic change in the country whereby the minority Maronites have lost control to Shiite Muslims and Druze. Israel still has an alliance with the Maronites, but they have been hard pressed to disassociate themselves from the Israelis as the price for retaining partial power. President Amin Gemayel yielded to Syrian and non-Maronite Lebanese influence and abbrogated the 1983 treaty with Israel. The Maronites were also forced to close the Israeli liaison bureau, which operated in the Christian sector near Beirut but kept open the Lebanese Christian Agency in Jerusalem headed by Pierre Yazbeck, a well-known advocate of Israel.

The situation in southern Lebanon is more difficult. Approximately 24,000 Israeli troops, which face 60,000 Syrian soldiers in the Bekaa Valley, are attempting to prevent renewed PLO infiltration and local resistance. According to Israeli intelligence reports, more than 2,000 guerrillas have returned via the Bekaa since their expulsion in 1982. The IDF has made a number of incursions north of the Awali to defend Christian targets.

The most serious threat to the IDF comes from the radicalization of the Shiites, who constitute a majority of the estimated 700,000 people who live in the South. Local Shiite clergy have taken the lead in promoting anti-Israeli sentiments. The Shiite Mufti in Lebanon, Shaikh Muhammad Mahdi Shamseddin, issued a _fatwa_ — a religious ruling — ordering comprehensive civil resistence against Israel. A number of small terrorist groups operate against the IDF: Hizballah (the Party of God), Junud Allah (the Soldiers of God) and Islamic Amal which seceded from the Amal party. All of them are somehow affiliated with Iran. There are also two tiny leftist Shiite groups which carry out attacks in the south: the Organization for Communist Action in Lebanon and the Lebanese Communist Party.

Because of the heavy human and financial toll, the IDF has been contemplating withdrawal. The lack of a central Lebanese authority to safeguard the South against a revival of the PLO makes this option difficult. Leaving Lebanon without security arrangements would be interpreted as a sign of weakness and negate the justification for the war. One policy pursued by Israel is to strengthen the South Lebanese Army headed by General Antoine Lahad. According to Shamir, the South Lebanese Army, an institutionalized substitute for the former Haddad forces, has made progress in training and organization. The first group of officers in the SLA has graduated from a special training program run by the IDF.

The National Unity Government in Israel announced that it plans to withdraw the IDF from Lebanon in a few months. It no longer insists on a simultaneous Syrian withdrawal from Lebanon as a condition for its own pullout. It is unclear, however, whether the government will be able to agree upon and achieve other conditions permitting a prompt and total withdrawal. Delays and partial withdrawals remain likely.

5.2 PEACE PROCESS WITH EGYPT.

Relations with Egypt, which reached their lowest point during the war in Lebanon, have not improved perceptibly. Egypt has not returned its ambassador to Tel-Aviv and the dispute over the Taba border is still pending. High-level talks in early 1984 failed to improve commercial and tourist ties between the two countries, which remain virtually frozen.

Moreover, Israeli intelligence alleges that Egypt has utilized the "cold peace" to modernize its defense forces (albeit under American auspices). The Egyptian army will soon have 12 divisions, an increase of about 20 percent. The tank corps have been westernized to include M-GOA-3 battle tanks and M-113 armored personnel carriers. The Air Force is converting to American F-5 and British jet fighters, while the Chinese and North Koreans are maintaining the Soviet weapons systems. Ehud Barak, Head of Military Intelligence, also claims that the Egyptians are preparing the infrastructure for a possible deployment of two armies in the Sinai. According to his estimates, Egypt may be getting ready militarily to rejoin the confrontation states.

Israel also seems worried about the cautious moves to renew ties between Egypt and the Soviet Union. More generally, the Israeli executive elite have refrained from overtly criticizing these developments. The estimate in Israel is that, for the time being, Egypt will try to keep the lowest possible profile in its relations with Israel, but abstain from activities which would jeopardize U.S. aid or the peace treaty itself.

5.3 MODERATE ARAB STATES. Israel's relations with moderate Arab states have improved in the past two years. The most dramatic indication of this trend was the recently convened conference of Moroccan Jews under the auspices of King Hassan. The Israeli delegation included Knesset members and other prominent leaders of the Moroccan Jewish community in Israel. The recent agreement between Morocco and Libya may these relations.

Israel has also maintained low-key contacts with Jordan. One of the issues is the ongoing problem of sharing Jordan River water resources. Another is the Jordanian plan to build a 1,500 MGW facility in Akaba, which, according to Israel would have an adverse ecological impact across the border in Eilat. Israel has apparently tacitly approved arms shipment to Iraq through Akaba and may consent to the Jordanian plans to build a pipeline for Iraqi oil to replace the pipeline closed down by Syria. Although King Hussein is unhappy about Israeli policy in the West Bank and Israeli air force and naval operations off Eilat, which allegedly infringed Jordanian territorial rights, Jordan is not likely to go beyond mild protests. The Jordanians have become increasingly alarmed by a build-up of pro-Syrian PLO forces led by Abu Musa at Deraa on Jordan's northern border. Jordan alerted the Americans of the danger ot a Syrian attack patterned on the Syrian invasion of Jordan during the civil war in 1970-71. At that time, the Syrians were dissuaded by an Israeli military alert instigated by the Americans.

5.4 OTHER ISLAMIC STATES. The Iran-Iraq war accelerated the revival of ties between Israel and Iran. According to various sources, Israel has sold Iran quantities of arms, ammunition, and spare parts. Early contacts were conducted directly between Israeli and Iranian officials, and, among others, the Swiss embassy in France. More recent arms deals are apparently conducted through private Israeli suppliers. Israel has been interested in the continuation of a low-level Gulf war; hence it supplies Iran and tacitly approves the transfer of arms to Iraq through Akaba. A prolonged conflict would weaken both Iran and Iraq and prevent them fron turning against Israel. The conflict has so far prevented the fundamentalist Shiite revolution from spreading in the region, a development which would endanger both Israel and moderate Arab regimes.

5.5 RADICAL ARAB REGIMES. There are no basic changes in Israeli policy towards the radical Arab states and especially Syria. The official view in Israel is that the long-term goals of Syria have not changed; it will strive to destroy Israel given the right set of political and military circumstances. In the interim, Syria will try to achieve strategic parity with Israel. To this end, it has been equipped with an ultra-modern Soviet weapons system, including the SA5 missile and the MIG-29. There are also some 7,000-9,000 Soviet advisers who man these systems and train the Syrian army. The advisers, who operate through the battalion level, are viewed as a potentially stabilizing force. The Soviets have consistently warned the Syrians against initiating military action against Israel, and have denied Syrian requests for weapons systems that would give Damascus a credible offensive capability.

According to Israeli intelligence sources, Syria will not embark on any military venture before the power struggle over President Assad's succession is settled.

5.6 THE UNITED STATES. American-Israeli relations, which reached a nadir during the war in Lebanon have improved dramatically. Israel and the United States have now formalized the strategic cooperation, first agreed upon in November 1981 but subsequently suspended. The American military and foreign policy establishment has thereby accepted the long-standing Israeli argument that Israel is a strategic asset in the Middle East, comparable to NATO in Europe or South Korea in Asia.

In this view, Soviet expansion in the Middle East is highly probable. Russian refusal to withdraw from Afghanistan, in spite of heavy casualties, and its presence in Syria are seen as manifestations of this resolve. The American decision makers have been influenced by the specter of a highly destabilized Middle East. Interregional conflicts, such as the Gulf War, illustrate the vulnerability of the oil routes and of the Arab states that protect them. The alleged refusal of Saudi Arabia to let U.S. forces use the Dhahran base and a similar Egyptian denial of the Ras Banas base on the Red Sea have made Israel an option for logistic basing of the American Rapid Deployment Force.

A destabilized Middle East has proven a fertile ground for terrorist activity in the name of many causes. As the bombings of the American embassy and the Marine contingent in Beirut demonstrated, the United States is vulnerable to such activity because of domestic political pressure to withdraw from high risk areas. It is significant that the rapprochement with Israel coincided with the major U.S. offensive against global terrorism. William J. Casey, the CIA director, hinted that some elements of the Israeli model of retaliation against terrorist attacks may be adopted by the United States.

The Reagan Administration was upset at the refusal of moderate Arab countries, especially of Jordan's King Hussein to accept the Reagan peace initiative of September 1982. Both the United States and Israel share the view that the pro-Arafat PLO is too weak to make a credible presentation of the Palestinian case. According to some estimates, King Hussein became even more hesitant to join negotiations on the West Bank. Other sources point out that the Arab states recently rejected a new secret peace proposed by the Secretary-General of the United Nations.

The recent cooperation between Israel and the United States is wide ranging. It includes increased economic aid, joint military exercises, purchase of some RPVs by the Navy, cooperation on intelligence and joint development of weapons systems, such as the Lavi aircraft and the missile boat Saar-V. Initial American approval has also been given to a free trade zone between the United States and Israel, making Israel the first country to enjoy such status.

5.7   THE WEST EUROPEAN COUNTRIES. There has been some improvement in relations with western Europe. Because of the increase in oil supplies and the disintegration of the PLO, most of the west European countries have moved away from the spirit and letter of the Venice Declaration, which pledged support to Palestinian independence. The recent visit of Chancellor Helmut Kohl to Israel improved relations with West Germany. However, Israel still strenuously objects to German plans to sell arms to Saudi Arabia. Relations with Great Britain are moderate, although Israel is known to have supplied Argentina with arms during the Falkland war. Former Defense Minister Arens proposed to Britain joint development of arms systems. Relations with France are generally good, although the French Socialists have given some nominal support to the Palestinian cause. Israel tends to attribute the more favorable climate in Europe to the decline in the importance of OPEC.

5.8 THE SOVIET UNION. There is a certain ambivalence in the current Soviet-Israeli relationship. On the one hand, Israel, by emphasizing its strategic importance in the Middle East, has committed itself to an unequivocal anti-Soviet stand. This constitutes a dramatic change from the traditional Labor foreign policy, which was emphatically opposed to setting Israel up as an anti-Soviet crusader. The Israelis also perceive that the Soviets have became more active in the Middle East. The rearming of Syria and the proposal to provide both Iraq and Syria with nuclear facilities are cited as examples of this policy.

On the other hand, there is an awareness that Soviet moves may be at least partially motivated by efforts to preserve some credibility with Iraq and Syria. Russian caution is especially noteworthy in view of the fact that the Soviet Union was humiliated by Syria when Assad refused to follow its plea on behalf of Arafat. Israeli sources argue that the Soviet Union lacks credibility in the Middle East because it has no links with Israel. Israelis have been encouraged by informal contacts with the Soviets and believe that the Soviet Union would like to increase its leverage in the Middle East by having some access, albeit indirect, to Israel.

5.9 LATIN AMERICA. Israel's traditional links with Latin America have become especially cordial in the past few years. For the past decade Israel has been exporting arms to Central American countries, including Guatemala and Honduras. According to some estimates, total sales in 1984 are expected to reach $22 million. There are also persistent rumors that Israel has supplied El Salvador and the contras in Nicaragua with arms. One theory holds that the CIA used Israel in order to "launder" help to the contras and the El Salvadoran government.

Both the Israeli government and the CIA have denied these allegations. Independent verification is lacking, yet it is pointed out that the allegations are at least logically plausible. Both Libya and the PLO are on record as supplying arms to Central American insurgents. The PLO helped train the Sandinistas before they overthrew the regime of Anastasio Somoza. Libya provided both financial and military help to the Sandinistas in Nicaragua and to the Farabundo Marti, which is the umbrella organization of five guerilla groups operating in El Salvador. El Salvador, either in recognition or anticipation of Israeli help, moved its embassy to Jerusalem. Costa Rica is the only other country to recognize Jerusalem as Israel's capital.

David Kimche, the Director General of the Israeli Foreign Ministry, has emphasized that Israel is interested in expanding technological aid to the region. Such a program would be patterned on Israeli experience in Black Africa in the 1960s.

5.10 ASIA. With the exception of Taiwan and Sri Lanka, Israeli relations with Asia are stagnant. In June 1984 the Foreign Minister of Sri Lanka acknowledged that his country was receiving some military aid from Israel to counter Tamil insurgents. Tamils have received support from the PLO and Libya. In spite of pressure from Muslim countries in the region, Sri Lanka may establish diplomatic relations with Israel.

5.11 BLACK AFRICA. For the past few years the Likud Government has tried to revive Israel's ties with Black Africa. Unofficial commercial relations have never been severed; Israeli companies and advisers operated in most of these countries even after diplomatic relations were broken. However, only two countries — Zaire and Liberia — have re-established formal relations with Israel.

6.
ISRAEL'S POLICIES IN THE OCCUPIED TERRITORIES

6.1 BACKGROUND. The territories occupied by Israel in 1967 include the Sinai and Gaza Strip, the West Bank and Old Jerusalem, and the Golan Heights. Sinai has been returned to Egypt, Old Jerusalem and the Golan Heights have been annexed outright, and the status of the West Bank and Gaza remains undecided. From the perspective of international law, with the exception of Sinai, these all remain occupied territories subject to the provisions of international law as found primarily in the Geneva Conventions.

During the Labor government, there was no clear policy with regard to the West Bank. Limited self rule was instituted and elections for the local municipalities were allowed in 1972 and 1976. Israel's settlement policy followed roughly the Allon Plan, which emphasized the primacy of security considerations. Ordinance No. 25 made it illegal for Jews to buy land in the West Bank and Gaza. Yet the progressively weakened Labor governments were subject to pressure from Gush Emunim and other elements, who viewed the West Bank as part of the historical-religious heritage of Israel. The map of the 27 settlements which were built between 1967 and 1977 reflects all these considerations. Seventeen settlements were built in the Jordan Rift valley and near the Dead Sea, and 5 in the Gush Etzion area, as stipulated by the Allon Plan. One was built in the Latrun region, to be included within the Roger's Plan of minor territorial adjustment. The remaining 3, and most notably Kiryot Arba near Hebron, were located in heavily populated areas of the West Bank (Judea and Samaria) as a result of Gush Emunim pressure.

6.2 LIKUD'S SETTLEMENT POLICY. At the end of 1977, a few months after Likud came to power, the new government changed the long-standing Labor policy and approved the establishment of Jewish settlements in all parts of the West Bank. In 1978 it was decided that settlements should be built only on public land, but Ordinance No. 25 was subsequently abolished and Jews were allowed to buy private land as well.

Following the policy change, the Attorney General's office and the Ministry of Justice were charged with preparing a comprehensive survey of public land in the West Bank. There are various interpretations as to what constitutes public land — a vague legal concept with ambiguities dating back to the Ottoman period. According to sources in the Ministry of Justice and the Ministry of Agriculture, about 1.7 million dunums of the seven million dunums of land in the West Bank were designated by Israel as public land (4 dunums = 1 acre). So far, about 300,000 dunums have been confiscated by the Israeli government. In addition, about 30,000 dunums have been purchased by individual Israelis from individual Palestinians. There were plans for the government to confiscate an additional 400,000 dunums in the future. The Ministry of Agriculture is officially responsible for supervising the settlement drive. Michael Dekel, the Deputy Minister of Agriculture who was personally in charge of the project, submitted a plan in 1982 which called for 100,000 Jews to be settled in the West Bank by the end of the decade. To accomplish this goal, urban settlements were to be built offering subsidized housing to attract settlers.

In 1983 Mattityahu Drobles, the Head of the Settlement Department of the World Zionist Organization presented a 30-year master plan for the Development of Judea and Samaria. The plan envisaged 165 settlements and a population which would reach parity with the estimated one million Arabs in the area. This estimate was later downgraded to 400,000 Jews by the year 2,000 and 530,000 in 2010.

There is widespread agreement both within the Likud and outside that these goals cannot be met at the present rate of development. However, there is no consensus as to whether the de facto annexation is still reversible. In a 1984 report, Meron Benvenisti, a specialist on the West Bank, argued that in terms of the Jewish infrastructure, the annexation is not reversible. He believes the number and the location of the settlements would make it very difficult for any Israeli government to negotiate over the West Bank.

The geographer and regional development specialist Elisha Efrat recently demonstrated that, in numerical terms, the Jewish settlement drive is a failure. Since the Six Day War, 112 settlements were built with a population of 23,000 (exclusive of the Jordan Valley). Jews represent only 3.5 percent of the Arab population of 800,000, settled in more than 450 villages and towns.

Most of the Jewish settlers and settlements are in the vicinity of the Green Line and Gush Etzion. This number amounts to only 1,750 settlers a year. On the average, the Arab population grows seven times faster than the Jewish population.

6.3 GENERAL LIKUD POLICY TOWARD THE PALESTINIANS. The Likud policy towards the Palestinians has changed a number of times. At the most general level, it had two goals. First, to encourage voluntary Palestinian emigration from the West Bank in order to diminish the "demographic threat." Government sources point out that the pace of Palestinian emigration has increased in recent years, and that 84,000 people departed between 1974 and 1980. It was hoped that attractive land prices would tempt many to sell out and leave. These projections are partly borne out by statistics. The approximately 800,000 Palestinians in the West Bank in 1983 constitute an increase of 138,000 over the 1976 figures. There are 476,000 Palestinians in the Gaza Strip.

However, a 1984 report of the Bank of Israel indicates that the trends which generated a low level of population increase in the 1970s are being reversed. In the 1981-82 period, the rate of annual increase was 2.1 percent compared to 1.9 percent in the late 1970s. This growth rate is explained by two factors. One is the increase in the birth rate. The total live birth rate for Israel was 23.6 in 1981; the combined live birth rate for the West Bank, Golan and Gaza area for the same year was 45.7, almost twice that of Israel. The second factor is a decline in the rate of emigration from the West Bank, which is attributed to the decline in the economy of the Gulf States. The decline in emigration, coupled with the fact that 69 percent of the population in the occupied territories is less than 24 years old, may increase future fertility rates.

The second goal of Likud policy was to keep the Palestinians quiescent in the face of de facto annexation. This goal was complicated by the presence of Jewish settlers, which increased the level of friction. During the tenure of Ezer Weitzman as Defense Minister, the official policy was viewed by Israelis as quite liberal. This perceived leniency prompted the Gush Emunim settlers to initiate a vigillante movement. The Jewish terrorist organization which is implicated in the attacks on West Bank mayors in 1980, the murders in the Islamic college in Hebron in 1983, and similar activities are an outgrowth of this movement.

6.4 SHARON'S HARD LINE. The tenure of Ariel Sharon and his chief-of-staff, Raphael Eitan, brought a radical change in the treatment of the Arab population. Sharon and Eitan sought to achieve quiescense through a hard-line approach towards protesters and demonstrators, a purge of PLO supporters throughout the West Bank, and the establishment of Village Leagues to collaborate with Israeli authorities. The Village Leagues were permitted considerable patronage and became part of the local administration in the West Bank. The Sharon-Eitan policy was responsible for some of the worst excesses of the military government's rule in the West Bank. It also proved to be counterproductive in quelling unrest. According to some statistics, the number of violent clashes increased during this period – in 1981-82 the number of incidents increased 117.6 percent over the previous year. The number of civilian disturbances increased from 2,467 in 1981 to 4,417 in 1982.

Moshe Arens, who became the Defense Minister in 1983, reversed the "strong-arm" policy of his predecessor. Under his "enlightened occupation," the Village Leagues were demoted and the military government was forced to observe more stringent law and order. Because of his alledged leniency, Arens came under repeated attacks from Jewish settlers who demanded stiff punishment for such infringements as stone-throwing and traffic hindrance. A recent ordinance provides for long prison terms for stone throwing. Arens and his military government moved away from traditional punishments such as blowing up the family homes of suspects. This punishment has proved ineffective as a deterrent and, because of its high visibility, has drawn international criticism. Arens also refrained from implementing the recommendations of a 1983 IDF panel which suggested exiling the offenders in civilian disturbances.

It is difficult to assess the effectiveness of the Arens policy on Palestinian behavior. The Palestinians have been generally subdued since the bitter struggle within the PLO and the split of the organization. Hussein's refusal to join the negotiations has left supporters of the Jordanian option with no political alternative.

6.5 NEW POLICY. The newly appointed Defense Minister Yitzhak Rabin is not expected to introduce major changes in the policies of the Military Administration. Prompted by American expressions of concern for the "quality of life" in the territories, the new government has authorized establishment of the first Arab bank to operate on the West Bank since 1967 and has considered appointment of

Arab mayors to replace Israeli army officers in charge of West bank municipalities since the ouster of elected mayors by the previous Likud government. At the same time, the military administration has renewed warnings to West Bank leaders against any attempt to resume political activities and issued new orders restricting the movement of West Bankers suspected of ignoring the warning.

Future behavior of the Palestinians will depend on a number of developments. First, the present demographic trends in the territories indicate a substantial increase in the younger population which has historically been a politically active group. The 13-25 age group has engaged in activities ranging from civil disobedience to terrorism.

Second, civilian unrest is normally related to the economic situation and structure of employment. The recession in Israel, the decline in emigration and the stagnation of the West Bank economy may reverse some of the growth trends of the 1970s. According to the Israel employment service, there were only 48,702 Palestinians employed in Israel in July 1984, compared with a high of 76,000 in 1981. The decline in emigration and the return of Palestinians from abroad has already caused a rise in the population aged 25-34. Further decline in emigration may increase the number seeking work in the population. Military government officials have recently reviewed contingency plans for public works programs in the occupied territories to combat the destabilizing affects of large-scale unemployment. Elements of these plans may be implemented should West Bank unemployment continue to grow.

According to the Bank of Israel report, the local economy on the West Bank has become stagnant. The industrial sector registered an annual average decline of 5 percent. Construction starts went down 8 percent and the number employed in industry decreased by 1 percent. Agricultural output declined 3 percent. Because of water quotas imposed by the Israeli authorities, only 5 percent of the agricultural land is irrigated; scarcity of water prevents the development of more efficient farming practices.

Third, the friction between the Jewish settlers and the local population has increasingly become a factor in the disturbance patterns. Stone throwing by the Palestinians, in order to disrupt the Jewish transportation network, is the focal point and has led to prolonged cycles of violence. In spite of stiff penalties, there has been no perceptible decrease in this activity. The second focal point of friction is the attempt by the Gush Emunim to establish a Jewish presence in the center of the Arab city of Hebron.

III. ECONOMIC ANALYSIS

1.
SUMMARY CONCLUSIONS

1.1 GENERAL CONDITIONS. The Israeli economy has been plagued in recent years by low growth and productivity, high and accelerating inflation, and a deepening balance of payments deficit. The adverse effects of these developments on the economy have been moderated by an institutional framework intended to shield the population, and by massive transfer payments from abroad. The new coalition has the opportunity to introduce the drastic reforms necessary to remedy Israel's long-standing problems, but formidable constraints remain.

1.2 PUBLIC FINANCE. The budget deficit has deepened with the rapid escalation of government spending (a reflection of increasing military expenditures and occupation costs). The increase in taxes has failed to keep pace. The deficit has been financed through monetization (which exacerbates inflation) and foreign transfers.

1.3 MANPOWER AND WAGES. Labor growth has slowed down in recent years. Labor supply in Israel is extremely sensitive to fluctuations in demand. Emigration has become a feasible option for many Israelis. There is a growing tendency to use Arabs from the Occupied Territories in menial, low-paying jobs. Wages in Israel are largely inflation-indexed. Wage differentials reflect social and educational differences, as well as political factors.

1.4 BALANCE OF PAYMENTS. Exports have become more diversified in recent years; in particular, military exports (mostly to Third World countries) are becoming a major factor. Imports have increased sharply, a reflection of high oil prices and the limited scope for import substitution. Tourism is cultivated as a source of foreign exchange. A crucial source of foreign exchange remains foreign transfer payments, primarily foreign aid and contributions channelled through various agencies.

1.5 AGRICULTURE. Agricultural output has increased, but the number of people employed in agriculture has declined steadily. Agriculture is increasingly dominated by unprofitable enterprises which require considerable government support.

1.6 INDUSTRY. Industry is plagued by problems, most notably inflation which diverts the attention of industrial managers. Generous subsidies, particularly for export industries, have resulted in industrial growth and diversification. An export-oriented military industry has blossomed, supplying a significant proportion of Israel's military needs and making Israel a major arms exporter.

1.7 CONSTRUCTION. The construction sector has been subject to massive swings. The government has played an instrumental role in the sector, particularly in providing subsidies for housing in the Occupied Territories. At the same time, there is a severe shortage of rental units in the major developed cities.

1.8 ENERGY. Israel is heavily dependent on foreign sources of energy. Energy costs have increased sharply in the past decade as oil imports have become more expensive. Israel is intensively seeking to develop alternative sources of energy.

1.9 FINANCIAL SECTOR. Israel's financial sector is characterized by considerable government intervention. Inflation is a major factor, determining the demand and supply of various credit instruments. The Bank of Israel is responsible for implementing monetary policy. It labors under serious constraints, not least of which is the necessity to monetize the large budget deficit.

2.
MACRO-ECONOMIC ANALYSIS

2.1 OVERVIEW OF THE ECONOMY. Since 1973, a year of escalating energy prices and mounting war costs, the Israeli
economy has experienced slow economic growth, low productivity, a deepening trade deficit, and an accelerating
rate of inflation. These developments are a result of two
main factors:

- a unique institutional structure that moderates the
  effect of external and internal shocks on individuals
  by spreading their effects over a long period;
- policy preferences which do not necessarily reflect
  purely economic considerations.

In recent years, the rate of inflation accelerated to
200 percent per year, then 400 percent, and then to 800
percent. There are indications that the yearly inflation
rate is now close to 1000 percent, one of the world's
highest. Despite this fact, inflation in Israel is not
the dominant issue, nor is it regarded as a particularly
dangerous phenomenon. The institutional structure enables
consumers, by indexation of wages, long-term savings, and
pensions, to keep up with inflation. Because of possible
social repercussions, Israeli policymakers refuse to take
measures which would halt inflation.

The balance of payments, rather than inflation, has
been Israeli policymakers' major concern. The balance of
trade deficit has been growing since the state was established. This deficit has been partly covered by foreign
loans, leading to an accumulation of heavy foreign debts
which might jeopardize the country's economic and political independence. The government has repeatedly undertaken restrictive policies to reduce the trade deficit
through either of the following:

- restrictive fiscal and monetary policies, aimed at
  curbing the growth in imports by reducing domestic
  absorption, while maintaining interest rates at a
  high enough level to discourage capital flight;

- direct (deliberately induced) or effective devaluation of the domestic currency (shekel), intended to increase the price of imports in domestic currency terms (making import substitutes more competitive), and to reduce the price of Israeli exports in foreign currency terms in overseas markets.

These policies have vastly different side-effects on the domestic economy. The first, restrictive (or deflationary) fiscal and monetary policy, tends to hinder economic growth, contribute to unemployment, and raise real interest rates. While curbing inflation, it is politically unpalatable. The second, devaluation of the shekel, is easier to enforce. Since the shekel was permitted to float freely by the Likud government, market forces reflect Israel's deteriorating trade deficit through an erosion in the purchasing power of the shekel. This exacerbates inflationary pressures, especially in an economy as open as Israel's.

2.2 EVALUATION AND PROSPECTS. The government has been unable to stem the worsening trade deficit. This failure apparently results from:

- lack of coordination among policy makers, mainly the fiscal and monetary authorities;
- reluctance to reorient the economy's productive structure, as that would have the immediate effect of increasing unemployment to a level the government regards as politically unacceptable.

Controlling inflation while creating conditions to improve productivity and strengthen the balance of payments could be achieved within Israeli economic constraints only by implementing an export-led growth plan. That requires a greater degree of government intervention in the market to insure rational capital allocation (which cannot occur automatically in a hyperinflationary situation). It also requires the promotion of new industries, the abandonment of those with limited market potential, and a greater penetration of international markets, especially important since the markets of most neighboring Arab states are closed to Israeli exports.

2.3 FACTORS FOR STABILITY AND INSTABILITY Because of its small size, Israel has a small market that cannot absorb internal or external shocks. In order to shield the public from economic shocks (energy crises, wars, stock exchange crises), the economy has generated a rigid institutional framework. This is composed of:

– the government;
– the Histadrut (the federation of trade unions);
– the National Institutions.

The function of this institutional framework is to moderate the impact of any crisis, insuring that the life of the average Israeli citizen does not become so intolerable as to encourage massive emigration.

The National Institutions are responsible for mobilizing money from external sources (other than foreign governments). The Histadrut, the primary trade union, is responsible for averting real wage erosion, while the government is responsible for insuring the smooth functioning of financial and labor markets. This institutional structure has generated almost full indexation of wages, financial assets and liabilities. It makes long-range planning possible, and insures that economic life goes on in the face of very high inflation.

On the other hand, because of indexation, inflation tends to perpetuate itself, and inflationary expectations are fueled at an ever-escalating rate. Because of government intervention, the allocation of capital in the financial market is inefficient, and economic signals are distorted. Meanwhile, disguised unemployment has been increasing.

Despite indexation, the inflationary process generates high costs for the Israeli economy. Price increases have been accompanied by relative price variability, and therefore have contributed to economic uncertainty. Inflation has encouraged excessive growth of the financial sector, especially commercial banks. Finally, high inflation defeats efforts to solve the balance of payments problem and to renew economic growth.

2.4 MACRO ECONOMICS AND ECONOMIC POLICY A major economic change occured in the Israeli economy in 1973. Until that year, the economy grew at an average rate of 10 percent per year, capital stocks and productivity rose at a substantial rate, and the inflation rate was single-digit. Since 1973, a year which saw Israel's involvement in an extremely expensive war and massive increases in energy costs, the rate of economic growth diminished to an average of 3 percent per year, capital stock increase and

productivity have both dropped to a low level, and inflation has accelerated at a maddening pace. Despite the
trends in the Israeli economy, the unemployment rate has
not changed significantly and has remained at a fairly low
level.

Following a trend beginning in the early 1970s, the
expansion of the principal sectors of the economy was led
by exports. Growth of export production during the 1970s
far surpassed that for the domestic market. This long-
term structural change in output destination stands out in
all the sectors of the economy apart from transportation,
where the growth rate was similar for both destinations.

Growth of Gross Domestic Product By Sector
in the Business Sector
(percentage)

	1960	1970	1981
Agriculture	10	9	10
Industry	22	29	30
Transportation & Communication	11	13	14
Construction	13	12	8
Trade & Services	44	37	38
Total Business Sector	100	100	100

Increase in Productivity by Period
(percentage increase)

	1960-65	1966-67	1968-72	1973-81	1960-81
Agriculture	6.7	8.6	5.6	6.1	6.3
Industry	13.4	-0.9	15.1	3.9	8.2
Transportation & Communication	10.3	0.0	15.5	3.9	7.7
Construction	11.0	-16.3	20.3	-1.8	4.5
Trade & Services	5.0	2.0	12.0	3.7	5.8
Total Business Sector	8.6	-0.7	13.6	3.4	6.6

The sharp decline of the growth rate since 1973 reflects in part a decrease in labor force growth and deteriorating investment performance. The critical factor in structural performance has been that consumption has fluctuated around a rising trend, while investments have fluctuated around a zero-growth trend. Real gross domestic capital formation is estimated to have been 5 percent lower in 1982 than in 1971, while real private consumption expenditure was 83 percent higher and real government consumption expenditure was 44 percent higher. The domestic demand variations were far greater than those of GDP which led to volatility in the balance of payments.

3.
BUDGET AND PUBLIC POLICY

3.1 BUDGET AGGREGATES. Government operations have contributed substantially to the demand imbalances in the Israeli economy. Over the years, government expenditures have increased enormously, both in absolute (real) terms and as a percentage of GNP. A large part of the increase in government spending has been in defense-related activity. Government spending in this area has entailed the following:

- maintaining a large standing army;
- acquiring weapons from foreign sources (though most arms transfers have been subsidized by foreign aid);
- the costs of military operations, notably the war in Lebanon, which has proved extremely expensive;
- occupation costs in the West Bank and Gaza, and, after 1982, in Lebanon as well.

Since the 1960s the weight of civilian government consumption has not changed but remains at about 10-12 percent of GNP. Non-civilian consumption rose from 10 percent to 25 percent of GNP. Policies concerning social and welfare services have resulted in rising expenditures, but in real terms they have not changed significantly.

Government budget revenue has increased substantially in relation to GNP but not sufficiently to eliminate or significantly reduce the budget deficit. The direct taxes weight in GNP rose from 17 percent in the 1970s to 26 percent in the beginning of the 1980s, the tax burden (taxes less subsidies and transfers) increased considerably.

3.2 BUDGET DEFICITS. A large proportion of the budget deficit has traditionally been financed by foreign resources. Virtually all of this has been in the form of grants or concessional foreign borrowing, and has been related in part to defense spending abroad.

Development of Main Budget Aggregates
(in percent of GNP)

	1978-79	1979-80	1980-81	1981-82
Budget Expenditure	66.2	70.2	68.2	72.6
Current Expenditure	58.9	61.3	60.4	64.1
Transfers/Subsidies	17.2	16.8	18.9	22.0
Interest Payments	8.6	6.9	8.4	11.1
Defense Expense	22.7	27.0	24.7	22.7
Capital Expenditure	7.3	8.9	7.8	8.5
Budget Revenue	47.1	50.8	53.2	49.7
of which: tax revenue	38.8	40.3	36.7	37.1
Budget Deficit	19.1	19.4	15.0	22.9
Foreign Grants	5.9	8.9	9.2	7.2
Foreign Borrowing	9.0	8.0	5.0	5.3
Domestic Bonds Issue	4.2	5.3	4.0	6.2
Net Credit from Bank of Israel	0.0	-3.3	-3.2	3.8
Net Impact on the Base Money	(0.8)	(-1.2)	(1.8)	(6.7)

The government budget deficit generated a liquidity injection to the economy and made it necessary to continue relying on a restrictive monetary policy. In countries with an efficient money and capital market, the principal monetary policy tool is open-market operations in government bonds. By buying or selling government bonds, the government and the central bank directly influence the monetary base and the public's assets portfolio mix. In Israel, however, the financial markets are too inflexible, so the Bank of Israel (the Central Bank) has focused on bank credit as its chief monetary instrument. This alone is incapable of countering the expansionary effect of the sizable government demand surplus. Since 1973, the financial assets held by the public have risen to accommodate the inflationary process in Israel.

3.3 PUBLIC ASSETS. The main monetary phenomenon in both 1981 and 1982 was the substantial real expansion of public holdings of financial assets. The high rate of inflation

encouraged the public to shift to linked (indexed) financial assets. At the end of 1982, more than three-quarters
of the wide aggregate liquid financial assets (M4) were
linked to the consumer price index or the exchange rate.
The bulk of M4 was, therefore, beyond the direct influence
of monetary policy. The aim of monetary policy is to
limit the growth of bank credit to the private sector to
less than the rate of inflation. This aim was achieved
betwwen 1980 and 1982 after the authorities introduced
quantitative ceilings on credit and other measures. In
1982 the Bank of Israel took steps to increase public
holdings of unlinked shekel assets. These policy changes
lay the groundwork for enhancing the role of monetary
policy in the future.

In 1982 and 1983, as a result of the war in Lebanon,
the government domestic consumption rose rapidly and the
government was forced to offset the expansionary effect by
imposing new taxes on the public and increasing the rate
of the value added tax.

Financial Assets of Public
(billion IS; end of period)

	1977	1978	1979	1980	1981	1982
Liquid Assets (M4)	7.7	12.2	22.3	55.3	105.2	241.1
Money Supply (M1)	1.9	2.7	3.5	7.0	12.5	25.5
Time Deposits	0.5	0.6	0.8	2.5	8.2	32.3
Foreign Currency/						
Linked Deposit	1.7	4.0	9.2	22.4	45.4	98.9
Tradable Gov't						
Bonds	3.6	4.9	8.6	23.4	39.1	84.4
Medium-Term Assets	9.8	16.3	33.5	96.2	244.6	817.1
Shares	2.7	4.7	8.1	36.2	108.8	482.0
Deposits	3.3	5.0	10.0	19.6	37.5	84.1
Savings Schemes	3.7	6.4	14.5	37.2	90.5	233.3
Long-Term Linked						
Deposits	0.1	0.2	0.9	3.2	7.9	18.5
Total	17.5	28.5	55.8	151.5	349.8	1,058.2

3.4 MACRO-ECONOMIC PROBLEMS. The macro-economic problems
the Israeli economy has faced since 1973 have gone from

bad to worse during the last two years. The combination
of high inflation — around 200 percent a year for a prolonged period, but now nearing 1,000 percent — coupled
with low economic growth — GNP increased by about 1 percent — resulted in a gaping current account deficit in the
balance of payments and a massive external debt (estimated
at about $23 billion).

Until the early 1980s, the major preoccupation of
Israeli policymakers was the balance of payments problem.
In 1982, concern shifted to inflation. The chief stimulus
was to lag the exchange rate behind the rate of inflation.
This policy failed — the current deficit in balance of
payments went up while inflation increased substantially.
Since the end of 1983 the policymakers have reverted to
the conventional policy focusing attention on the balance
of payments and economic growth. They agreed that, in
order to achieve structural change in the economy, government expenditure had to decrease, releasing resources
for investments and exports. After initial implementation
of this policy, exports increased as did the rate of the
economic growth, but inflation became much worse.

3.5 NEW POLICY DIRECTIONS. The coalition government formed
in 1984 is seen by most Israelis as offering perhaps the
last opportunity for substantial economic reform. The
Labor Party, which for years has been accusing the Likud
government of overspending, is in a position to enact
larger budget cuts, without fear of the opposition (which
is still part of the government) taking political advan-
tage of the unpopularity of austerity measures. There is
a limit to how far austerity measures can go:

- Spending on defense cannot be cut substantially unless the government succeeds in extricating itself
  from its costly occupation of Lebanon.
- Both major parties have an eye on political support
  should the current government dissolve. For that
  reason, there is little likelihood of budget cuts
  penalizing special interests (particularly religious
  groups) too severely, as their support is instrumental. Similarly, revenue-boosting measures that would
  offend religious sentiment (such as allowing the
  national airline, El Al, to fly on the Sabbath) can
  only be enacted at the risk of antagonizing religious
  groups.

- The substantial subsidies to the kibbutzim, which are economically unprofitable, and also to West Bank settlements, are not likely to be cut, in view of the great political sensitivity these issues carry.
- As long as a state of war, and, more importantly, a war mentality persist, Israel cannot be managed fiscally as a "normal" country. Too many facets of life are affected by the war atmosphere: pressures of ever-escalating defense-spending, the need to maintain all able-bodied adult males in uniform for up to 45 days a year, and both the direct and indirect costs of continued occupation.

4.
MANPOWER AND WAGES

4.1 DEMOGRAPHIC FACTORS. Population growth has slowed sigificantly in recent years because of the decline in immigration. Labor force growth decreased from 4.0 percent in 1978 to 3.2 percent in 1980 and 1.3 percent in 1982. One of the striking features of the Israeli economy is the cyclical sensitivity of the labor supply, which is much greater than in other countries. Specifically, when the demand for labor in Israel is sluggish, the rate of immigration declines and the rate of emigration rises. Consequently, a fall in the demand for labor has less impact on the unemployment rate and a larger effect on the labor supply than elsewhere. The fluctuation in the demand for labor generates swings in the number of workers from the "administered" areas. Their year-to-year growth rate has been markedly sensitive to cyclical conditions, with the employment base concentrated in construction, agriculture, and industry.

4.2 COMPOSITION OF LABOR FORCE. The composition of the labor force reflects the structure of Israeli society, which is remarkably heterogeneous for the country's size. Some clearly identifiable groupings exist, namely:

- "Mainstream" Jewish workers, who are uncommitted to any particular religious or political ideology. These dominate the government bureaucracy and the upper and middle management levels of private industry.
- Agricultural workers on kibbutzim, all of whom are Jewish. They are committed to a way of life which tends to be (but is not always) collectivist and socialist. In view of the small size of the kibbutzim, labor employed there is generally not very productive.
- Members of numerous religious and/or secular Jewish groupings with a strong ideological overtone. While

small in number, they are of major political significance, as they constitute the mainstay of the settler movement in the occupied territories. Heavily dependent on government subsidies, they are particularly unproductive.

- Arab citizens of Israel. In principle, they are permitted to work in all sectors. In practice, they are barred from positions with security connections (of which there are many in Israeli industry). Differentials in student/teacher ratios in Arab and Hebrew education, and the relative dearth of facilities in Arab schools have led to Arab educational standards far behind those of Jewish citizens of Israel. As a consequence, they tend to be employed in lower-paying jobs, as factory or construction workers, in agriculture (usually on a seasonal basis) or in the lower echelons of the government bureaucracy (if they speak Hebrew). A significant number of Israeli Arabs are engaged in small business.
- Arabs from the occupied territories, about 90,000 of whom commute to work in Israel. These are not Israeli citizens, speak little or no Hebrew, and are not permitted to reside in pre-1967 Israel. They are typically employed in very low-paying (relative to Israeli citizens) menial and factory jobs. They do not belong to the Histadrut and have few rights. They may not legally stay overnight in pre-1967 Israel, although some do so illegally.

The above outline does not capture all the nuances of the Israeli labor market. The Jewish labor force can be further subdivided into Ashkenazim (Jews of Eastern European origin), Sephardim (Jews of Spanish and North African origin), and Oriental Jews (Jews from Arab countries outside of North Africa). The last two groups complain of a racist bias against them, although they already constitute a majority within the Jewish population. They are generally less well educated and usually hold lower-paying jobs.

Recent Jewish immigrants (mostly from Eastern Europe) are naturalized immediately, but it takes them time to become fully adjusted and to master modern Hebrew. They rely heavily on government support until they have completed their adjustment process, and so contribute economically.

The non-Jewish population includes a large number of Druze, who are Arabic-speaking but are not considered Arabs by the Israeli authority. They serve in the Israeli

Israeli Labor Force: Selected Data
(thousands)

	1978	1979	1980	1981	1982
Average Population	3,693	3,786	3,878	3,948	4,023
Working-Age Population	2,532	2,596	2,661	2,709	2,757
Civilian Labor Force	1,255	1,277	1,381	1,349	1,367
Israeli Employed	1,213	1,241	1,255	1,280	1,289
Employed from the Administrated Areas	71	77	75	76	79
Unemployed	42	37	64	68	68
Employed in Public Services	350	362	368	377	381
Employed in Business Sector	934	956	962	979	996
Participation Rate*	49.6	49.2	49.5	49.8	49.6
Unemployment Rate*	3.6	2.9	4.8	5.1	5.0

* = percentages

army, and have more economic opportunities than most Israeli Arabs.

The heterogeneous composition of the labor force presents certain problems. It is linked to the fragmentation of Israeli society, although more as a symptom than as a cause. It reduces the flexibility of the economy, inasmuch as it limits the substitutability of labor. Furthermore, to the extent that wage distribution stems from cultural and political factors rather than exclusively economic ones, it leads to gross misallocation of human resources.

4.3 WAGES. Wage behavior in Israel is dominated by centralized wage-fixing institutions. The most important of those is wage indexation, which provides for automatic cost-of-living adjustments to wages. The second component of wage-determinism in Israel is an agreement between the Employers' Federation and the Histadrut that the level of real wages will be maintained. The third component consists of specific agreements made of the sectoral, industrial, or plant level, depending on particular conditions.

The rigidity of the wage structure, while it minimizes the havoc caused by hyperinflation, has serious drawbacks. It prevents the labor market from responding efficiently to new opportunities, and slows down the adjustment in relative wages to reflect an evolution in the productivity of a particular class of labor. It also perpetuates discrimination inherent in the existing wage distribution, and particularly penalizes workers (especially Arabs) who are either not members of the Histadrut or have little voice in it.

5.
BALANCE OF PAYMENTS

5.1 THE CURRENT ACCOUNT DEFICIT. Israel has a large and persistent current account deficit. Imports reached $9.6 billion in 1983 while exports amounted only to $5.1 billion. In the course of its brief history, Israel has been able to mobilize large sums in the form of unilateral transfers that have financed almost two thirds of the trade deficit. These unilateral transfers consisted of:

- Foreign aid from Israel's allies, notably the United States. Aid from the United States has come to be a major factor not only in Israel's current account balance, but in financing government operations as well. Total U.S. aid to Israel stood at an estimated $2.4 billion in 1983-84, although there is some disagreement in U.S. government circles about the actual total figure that should be computed. U.S. aid to Israel includes military aid (to finance military purchases from American producers) and economic aid (administered by Israeli officials with minimal interference from USAID officials).
- Charitable contributions, mostly from Jewish groups abroad. These are often earmarked for a specific purpose, like the building of a hospital or planting trees. They result in an infusion of foreign exchange and relief of fiscal pressure on the government. In nearly all instances, donations channeled through charitable institutions are tax exempt in the country of origin.
- Reparations to war victims remitted by the Federal Republic of Germany both to the Israeli government and to individual Israeli citizens. These reparations were a major source of foreign exchange in the early years of Israel's existence.
- Remittance to Israelis by relatives (not all of them Israelis living abroad) from foreign countries.

The remaining part of the current account deficit has been financed by foreign loans and investments. The large deficits of the last decade were covered by huge increments to Israel's foreign debt.

5.2 EXPORTS. As the economy of Israel developed, exports grew rapidly and became greatly diversified. Citrus fruit, which had been the major export, was replaced at first by polished diamonds and later by other industrial exports.

Military exports have become a major source of foreign exchange. Their growth stems from the rapid development of Israel's arms industry, and the growing market for weapons worldwide. Israel has proved particularly proficient at assembling weapons using parts manufactured in other countries (mostly the United States), then selling them to "pariah" states to whom Western producers would be embarrassed to sell arms directly — countries like South Africa and a number of South and Central American states. It is assumed that such activity meets with at least tacit acquiescence of the U.S.

Commodity Exports By Branch

	1955	1967	1975	1980
Total Exports (million $)	88	399	1.798	5.292
(percent)				
Citrus	36.7	17.8	9.8	4.4
Other Agricultural	2.3	3.7	5.6	6.1
Diamond	23.5	33.0	30.5	26.6
Other Industrial	37.5	45.4	54.1	62.9
Total	100.0	100.0	100.0	100.0

The geographic breakdown of commodity exports contains a striking feature: the increased share of the "other countries" category in the last decade. Part of this growth results from the inclusion in this category of goods not classified by country of destination (largely military equipment), but the same trend appears even when the unclassified group is excluded. The United States has been a major buyer of Israeli exports. Western Europe accounts for nearly half of all Israeli exports (the United Kingdom and West Germany being the major buyers).

The markets of LDC's have been penetrated by Israeli exports only to a limited degree; the major commodity they buy from Israel is weapons.

A major consideration determining the geogrpahic distribution of Israeli exports is political. Israel is officially boycotted by all of its Arab neighbors except Egypt, which bought only $1.1 million of Israeli goods in the third quarter of 1983. Many Third World countries maintain no diplomatic relations with Israel, and buy few Israeli exports. On the other hand, there is considerable illicit traffic between Israel and Lebanon, both within the Israeli-occupied zone and outside it. There are no official estimates of that trade, but it appears to involve both Israeli produce and manufactured goods. Israel imports little from Lebanon in exchange.

Geographic Structure of Exports
(% of Total)

	1965-69	1970-75	1975-80
United Kingdom	11.8	9.8	8.0
West Germany	9.5	8.9	8.9
Other EEC	18.3	19.1	19.7
Other Europe	19.2	14.5	12.9
United States	16.7	18.8	16.9
Other	24.5	28.9	33.6
Total	100.0	100.0	100.0

5.3 IMPORTS. Israel's civilian commodity imports have risen substantially in line with changes in import patterns. Due to a sharp increase in the cost of imported oil, the weight of imported production inputs has gone up at the expense of the other two items. The substantial weight of inputs in total imports reflects the small import substitution margin the country has. As a result, reduction of imported goods would directly affect production and employment levels. Thus, a path of positive economic growth requires an increase of imported goods and an export-led growth plan. In the past the government tried to stop import growth by a combination of strategies such as freezing economic growth, imposing restrictions on imports, and alternative exchange rate policies. In most years, government policy has been unable to change the composition of output in the direction of commodities with low import components.

The United States is Israel's major supplier. European countries (notably West Germany) account for a substantial proportion of Israeli imports. Japan, with extensive customer relationships elsewhere in the Middle East, sells relatively little to Israel. Imports of Egyptian goods are also negligible.

Civilian Commodity Import By Category

	1955	1965	1975	1980
	(million $)			
Total	337	730	4.135	7.857
	(percent)			
Consumer Goods	15.4	10.2	7.8	6.8
Investment Goods	23.0	21.8	16.0	12.1
Production Inputs	61.6	68.0	76.2	81.8
of which oil	(9.9)	(6.5)	(16.1)	(26.5)
Rough Diamonds	(9.9)	(6.5)	(20.6)	(14.0)
Total	100.0	100.0	100.0	100.0

5.4 SERVICES. Exports of tourism services (i.e. tourists coming to Israel) have tended to increase. Expenditure by foreign tourists is 30 percent higher than Israeli spending on tourism abroad. In 1982, tourism accounted for about 4 percent of the country's total exports.

Israel has become a major tourist center despite the political uncertainty of the region. This is largely a result of the following:

- The climate is agreeable year-round, with relatively little rainfall.
- Israel is close enough to Europe for Europeans to be able to travel there at little expense.
- With the shekel depreciating rapidly, foreign tourists are not affected by the high inflation rate, and generally find prices relatively low.
- A number of tourists come to visit religious and

archeological sites, including some sites not in Israel itself but in the occupied territories.
 — Despite the continuing tension in the region, it is easier now for tourists to combine visits to Israel with visits to equally enticing Arab countries. Travel between Israel and Egypt is now routine, and tourists are able to cross over from Jordan (legally) and Lebanon (illegally).

Since the 1960s, with rising prosperity and easing controls, Israeli tourism abroad has become a significant expenditure item. Despite a tax on foreign travel and the rapidly depreciating shekel, Israelis travel abroad in large numbers. This can be attributed to the following:

 — Proximity to Europe encourages travel there, especially during the hot summer months.
 — Many Israelis visit relatives and acquaintances in foreign countries, notably Europe, the United States and South Africa.
 — It is now easy for Israelis to travel to Egypt, and many are eager to do so.

Israel's large volume of international trade generates a substantial transportation expenditure. Exports and imports of transportation services are more than $1 billion each — exports reached $1.3 billion and imports $1.1 billion. Direct defense imports, mostly financed by the U.S. government, in recent years reached an average annual amount of $1.5 billion.

5.5 TRANSFER PAYMENTS AND CAPITAL FLOWS. Since the creation of the state, unilateral transfers have covered between 60 and 75 percent of the import surplus. Net long-term capital flows have almost always been considerably smaller than unilateral transfers, but this is not always clear-cut. Long-term capital flows may include a sizable grant component if interest charges or terms of repayment are more favorable than the prevailing market terms. There are three major sources of financing for the trade deficit: (1) the U.S. government; (2) world Jewry; and (3) the West German government.

The U.S. government has given Israel loans and grants through many specialized agencies. Net U.S. aid averaged some $1.7 billion annually in the 1973-1980 period. Although the share of grants and loans has fluctuated, official grants have amounted to approximately 60 percent of the total during this period. Adding the grant element of loans to outright grants, this share becomes 70 percent of total aid.

World Jewry supports Israel financially by donating funds or by buying Israeli government low-interest bonds. In recent years the annual amount from this source has been less than half a billion dollars; relative to the level of the import surplus, the decline is even greater. Nevertheless, the years 1967 and 1973 (when Israel was engaged in wars) are striking examples of the availability of this source when it is urgently needed.

The Federal Republic of Germany has provided Israel with reparations and personal restitution. The reparation payments ceased in 1965 and were replaced by loans. Personal restitutions have increased annually to almost $400 million in recent years.

Direct Foreign investment in Israel is very small in comparison with other capital inflows. By 1967 direct investments had grown to $120 million; they declined thereafter, and net receipts from this source have become negligible (negative) in recent years.

5.6 EXTERNAL DEBT. Israel's external debt has been growing rapidly in dollar terms in recent years. Gross external liabilities rose from $10 billion at the end of 1975 to $26 billion by the end of 1982. This is an increase from 87 percent to 117 percent of GNP. The overall maturity structure of Israel's external debt reflects its heavy reliance on direct borrowing from foreign governments. At the end of 1982, 70 percent of Israel's debt was long-term with the remainder split about equally between medium- and short-term. The forecast repayment structure of Israel's existing debt emphasizes the long-term nature of its liabilities. Thirty-seven percent is repayable after 1993; 17 percent from 1988 to 1992 and only 25 percent in the next year, most of which consists of short-term loans which will be renewed next year.

Despite the favorable maturity structure, the debt service ratio (the ratio of debt servicing to exports) is high in comparison with other developing nations, and the total debt per capita is the world's highest. Some relief of the debt burden derives from the fact that the United States, Israel's main creditor, periodically "forgives" substantial amounts of Israel's debt.

6.
AGRICULTURE

6.1 THE IMPORTANCE OF AGRICULTURE. Despite the stereotype of Israelis living on kibbutzim, engaging in collective farming, only a small percentage of agricultural output is produced by kibbutzim (which are encountering serious economic problems due to their relatively small size). Agriculture itself has never accounted for more than about one-tenth of total output; it is eclipsed by industry and services.

The early emphasis on agriculture stems to a large extent from early Zionist ideals. Herzl, the father of modern Zionism, envisaged a society in which Jews, long denied the opportunity to till the soil, redeemed themselves and the land of Palestine, generating a new breed: the Jewish farmer. A major function of Zionist institutions like the Jewish Agency was to acquire land for agricultural settlements. By the time the Jewish state was created in 1948, a modest percentage of its land area (approximately 9 percent) had passed to Jewish hands. Since then, the Zionist establishment has greatly expanded the scope of Jewish (state) ownership through appropriation of the land of exiled Palestinians, allocation of public land to Jewish agricultural use, confiscation, and legitimate land transfers.

The role of the agricultural sector has evolved substantially. While the bulk of the land continues to be held by the government or by public institutions, and the percentage of GDP contributed by agriculture has grown slightly, Israel has emerged as a country specializing in manufactured goods and in services – not unlike wealthier European countries of roughly of the same size.

Today, several features dominate the profile of the agricultural sector:

- The number of Jewish laborers involved in agriculture has diminished. As the lure of higher pay in other sectors has enticed many to change occupations, there is an increasing tendency to employ Arabs for seasonal agricultural labor – in violation of early Zionist ideals.

- As in many other countries, small-scale agricultural settlements (including many kibbutzim) are under increasing pressure. Many agricultural units are finding that salvation lies in increased emphasis on "agribusiness."
- A considerable proportion of farming undertaken by Jewish laborers is not undertaken for profit, but instead to promote a religious or secular ideology. This is especially true of settlements in the occupied territories, which are of negligible economic importance inasmuch as they produce little yet cost much.

6.2 PROFILE OF THE AGRICULTURAL SECTOR. In the last decade the share of agricultural production in the business sector has increased slightly to about 11 percent. On the other hand, the total number of persons employed in agriculture has decreased from nearly 100,000 in the early 1970s to about 85,000 in recent years, while the sector share of total employment has fallen to nearly 6 percent. These trends have to do with an overall productivity increase in agriculture, which, on the average, has been higher than in other sectors of the economy. This productivity increase has made it possible for agricultural production to grow while the number of people the sector employs has been reduced.

The distribution of agricultural output shows that since the early 1970s the share of field crops has almost doubled to nearly 21 percent, the share of vegetable production has remained at 10 percent, citrus production has dropped from 23 percent to about 16 percent, with livestock production declining from 41 percent in 1972 to about 35 percent in 1982.

The decline of livestock production in the total agricultural output reflects the low percentage contribution of exports. Almost all of the livestock products (milk, eggs and chickens, fish, livestock for meat) go to local consumption and face a small market.

Despite the drop in total production, the most important crop is still citrus fruit, earning about $250 million in exports. Emphasis is placed on import substitutes, such as cotton and grain and on sub-tropical fruits, vegetables, and flowers for export.

The general yearly water consumption in Israel is approximately 1,700 million cu m, three-quarters of which is for agricultural use. The cultivated area has slightly increased while the share of irrigated area has grown from about one-third in the early 1960s to nearly one-half of the cultivated area in recent years.

Cultivated Area in 1980 by Type of Locality
(thousand dunums)[*]

	Total	Kibbutz	Moshavim	Other Jewish	Non-Jewish
Crops (winter & summer)	2,593	1,214	661	154	564
of which irrigated	767	547	173	40	7
Vegetables	355	66	130	54	105
Fruit Plantation	866	156	336	233	161

[*] There are 436 thousand more dunums, 40 for fish ponds and the rest for auxiliary farms, flower nurseries, etc.

Agricultural Output Subsidies
Divided By Total Output Of Branch

Average	1970-77	1978	1979	1980	1981	1982
Eggs	17	26	33	13	20	36
Poultry-meat	12	30	19	15	31	45
Milk	33	43	55	9	40	58
Total Livestock	16	21	24	7	20	31
Crops	1	1	1	0	0	1
Total Subsidies	7	9	9	3	8	12

Price supports for agricultural products are paid as direct subsidies to farmers based on amounts of desirable crops produced.

It is hard to determine quantitively whether the main beneficiaries of the price supports have been the farmers or consumers, but there is no doubt that the subsidies improve the farmers' financial situation, and without such aid a crisis in agriculture would be almost inevitable.

6.3 FUTURE OF AGRICULTURE. The fundamental problem of Israeli agriculture is excess agricultural production capacity. The number of farmers has been determined primarily by socio-national considerations. The amount of land allocated to a person defined as a farmer is relatively small. To earn a "normal" income from a small area of land requires a large output, which generally implies the employment of capital-intensive techniques. Since there is presently no market for such a volume of output at prices that would justify the requisite capital investment and factor payments, farmers would suffer losses unless they were heavily subsidized. Some branches have been improved through heavy subsidies; others have become worse because of the relatively low amount of subsidies.

The future of the agricultural sector depends on a number of factors, many political. Politically motivated agricultural activities will remain a major factor in the Israeli scene for years to come, although their economic significance is likely to be slight. Regardless of economic pressures, kibbutzim will be maintained and continue to be subsidized by the government for propagandistic purposes. Israel will continue to apply advanced technology to agricultural production, although there are limits to how much can be accomplished through technology given other resource constraints.

The economic factors shaping the future of agriculture are also important. One factor of paramount importance is the water-supply situation. Israel has been depleting its water resources (and those of the occupied territories, especially the West Bank) at a rate well in excess of the renewal rate, resulting in dire consequences for the agricultural sector's future.

Other economic factors affecting agriculture include:

- the escalating price of agricultural land due to urban sprawl;
- the diminishing supply of immigrant labor and the growing propensity for Jewish citizens of Israel to work in other sectors than agriculture, which almost certainly suggests a growing role for Arabs in Jewish-held agricultural units;
- an uncertain future for Israeli produce markets in the EEC, as a result of the admission of Greece and the likely admission of Spain and Portugal to the Common Market, giving their produce preferential treatment in many markets now buying Israeli produce.

7.
INDUSTRY

7.1 PROFILE OF THE INDUSTRIAL SECTOR. Industrial production now comprises more than one quarter of the total production of the business sector. The number of persons employed in the sector rose to more than 110 thousand, which is about 23 percent of the total employed persons in the country. After services, industry is the most important sector for production and employment.

The striking fact about industrial sector development in recent years is that industrial growth has been heavily export-oriented. Nearly all branches contributed to the increase in the weight of exports. Metal products, arms production, and the electrical and electronic equipment industry made especially impressive gains in production and exports over the last decade. In line with the export-led production, there is a continuing shift in the structure of the economy toward high-technology production.

Among the industrial branches, two are quite different from the others: diamonds and non-civilian items. The diamond industry was set up largely because Israeli citizens possessed the necessary skills. Raw materials had to be imported (mostly from South Africa), and markets had to be developed overseas for the product. The Israeli diamond industry now has the highest volume of exports, and it captures a large portion of the world trade. In recent years, due to a sharp decrease in world demand, the diamond industry has been in serious crisis; production has dropped, and many workers have become unemployed.

7.2 MILITARY EXPORTS Military equipment is produced by many branches of industry, such as electronics, machinery, and transport equipment. In recent years, the weight of these goods in industrial exports has increased substantially and it is likely to have a long-range effect on the country's production and export growth. Such exports possess several notable advantages:

- A high growth capacity, eclipsing that of civilian industry.
- Excellent opportunities for export, providing partial relief of the foreign exchange problem stemming from the current trade deficit and the growing debt burden.
- The sophisticated nature of these products, in which local inventiveness and development are an important element.
- The positive impact they have on Israeli manufacturing in general and on industries supplying intermediates in particular.
- Military exports are presumably less vulnerable to short-term changes in export profitability and to competition from countries with cheap labor, since their success derives from technological achievements and the ability to capture an increasing slice of the world market.
- A diplomatic benefit: Israel's ability to maneuver is enhanced by the fact that it is a potential arms supplier. Israeli sales of weapons to South Africa, a state which is not generally able to obtain weapons elsewhere, has fostered close ties between the two countries. A quiet system of alliance has also been set up with countries in South and Central America, where Israel has acted as intermediary for U.S. weapons in addition to selling its own military equipment. Iran and Indonesia are also believed to have obtained weapons through Israel.
- A major political consideration is the extent to which Israel is less dependent on foreign suppliers of weapons. While Israel's massive military needs cannot be met through domestic production, growing self-sufficiency in arms production increases Israel's ability to resist diplomatic pressure from the United States.

At the same time, the growth of the arms industry in Israel has some drawbacks: once arms production reaches a scale necessitating massive exports (a point some believe has already been reached), changing political conditions worldwide pose a threat to the outlets Israel has cultivated for its military exports. The diplomatic factor may prove to be a two-edged sword; Israel may have to subordinate its foreign policy to trade considerations. Furthermore, Israel's self-professed image as a peace-loving nation is not enhanced by becoming a major arms supplier.

7.3 GENERAL CONDITIONS. Inflation has been accelerating rapidly in the past five years. Such a development has a negative effect on productivity. It makes planning quite difficult for manufacturers, who must adjust their purchases of raw materials and other factors of production to expected developments in these prices as well as the price of their own products. The sharpening of price fluctuations around a high trend increases the uncertainty facing manufacturers, and prompts them to slow down production and investment. Such developments have accentuated the effect of the rapid shift of production orientation from the local to overseas market.

The uptrend in exports of locally developed goods was accompanied by a steady rise in R&D grants. These grants increased by an annual average of 8 percent in real terms in the last six years.

Up to 1979 the government had supported industrial investors through so-called development loans which where not linked to the price index. Given the phenomenally high inflation rate, these loans have a major subsidy component which is increased through the escalation of inflation. The subsidies, which in part were anticipated, and during the 1970s significantly reduced the cost of capital to the manufacturer, led to a high rate of investment in that sector. The linkage of development loans in 1979 reduced the demand for that type of financing and prompted investors to mobilize capital through the stock exchange.

Tel Aviv and its environs form the main industrial center, with almost half of the total number of establishments employing about one third of the country's labor force. Many large enterprises are located near Haifa Bay and in the Negev. Another industrial growth center is being developed in the Ashdod-Ashkelon region.

Industrial Production and Exports by Branch

Branch	Production Indices			Exports	
	Weight	**1975**	**1982**	**1981**	**1982**
	(Base: Average 1978=100)			(U.S. $million)	
Total (except diamonds)	100.00	85	109	3.637	3.532
Mining/Quarrying	3.17	114	124	194	189
Food, Beverages, Tobacco	12.61	80	121	339	349
Textiles	6.96	84	102	110	93
Clothing	5.71	81	112	227	255
Leather	0.91	85	90	8	7
Wood	3.61	85	103	28	23
Paper	1.70	83	102	8	6
Printing/Publishing	3.86	73	112	21	20
Rubber/Plastic Products	3.82	82	100	108	107
Chemical/Oil Products	9.82	81	107	736	648
Non-metalic/Mineral Products	3.77	105	101	17	15
Basic Metal	2.56	92	78	59	36
Metal Products	14.56	90	111	464	515
Machinery	3.79	78	112	117	112
Electrical/Electronic Equipment	12.28	82	115	387	466
Transport Equipment	9.32	85	104	513	440
Miscellaneous	1.55	102	94	252	254

8.
CONSTRUCTION

8.1 THE DEMAND FOR HOUSING. In the long run the demand for housing for purchase is determined by a number of factors, among them:

- Demographic factors, like the population growth rate the rate of family formation, average family size and age distribution.
- Economic factors, like the growth of disposable income, the growth of community wealth.
- Social factors, like the attitudes toward home ownership, the strength of family ties.
- Financial factors, like the rate at which money can be borrowed to finance home purchases, tax treatment of homeowners, and the availability of housing subsidies through public financing.

Israeli society is unusually heterogenous, which adds a dimension to the demand for housing. Different ethnic and religious groups have vastly differing lifestyles; some favor an extended family structure, others value privacy. In certain areas, hostile relations between different communities have resulted in segregation of varying strictness. Discrimination in housing is not unusual and sometimes is tacitly promoted by government policy.

The tight supply of housing has led to housing shortages, notably in dwellings for middle-income families in large developed cities. As a result, rental units for such families are difficult to find; condominium purchases are a necessity for the middle class.

8.2 THE ROLE OF PUBLIC FINANCING. In the short run public financing has an important impact on demand. The role of the Ministry of Housing loans is, inter alia, to adjust the level of short-term demand to the supply level.

Generally, there have been sharp swings in public construction and relatively mild ones in private construction. In the 1979-82 period, public starts have held

Residential Construction by Initiating Sector
(thousands of units)

		Starts			Completions	
	Total	Private	Public	Total	Private	Public
1970-75	56.0	30.0	26.0	46.7	26.9	19.9
1976-78	31.0	22.5	8.4	44.6	24.0	20.6
1979-82	34.2	21.9	12.3	31.9	20.0	11.8

relatively steady. This stabilization reflects a change in the nature of public construction, which is becoming increasingly similar to private construction, shifting from the erection of housing estates directly under the aegis ot the Ministry of Housing to projects executed through private contractors with only minimal Ministry intervention. This intervention takes the form of overall planning, development of the infrastucture, allocation of land, and direct aid to the contractors — the partial financing of construction and commitment to purchase any unit they fail to sell. Residential construction initiated by the public sector is intended primarily for persons eligible for Housing Ministry aid, with the size of the units limited to 85 square meters.

An especially striking feature of public construction is the expansion of Jewish construction in the occupied territories, notably the West Bank. In 1979, starts of units numbered to 600, which in 1980 jumped to 1,800, in 1981 to 2,400, and in 1982 to 3,000. The policy of enticing people to settle in the occupied territories, making it more difficult for any future Israeli government to contemplate withdrawal from the West Bank, was vigorously promoted by the Likud government. It offered residential units in the West at bargain prices to Jewish citizens. A number of Jewish families opted to settle in the West Bank for economic reasons, and now have a strong stake in maintaining the Israeli presence there.

9.
ENERGY

9.1 ENERGY DEPENDENCE. Israel is almost entirely dependent on imported oil. Less than 2 percent of primary energy is produced domestically (crude petroleum natural gas, solar energy and oil shale). The ratio of total energy consumption to GDP remained almost the same over 1973-1982, compared to an average decrease of 31 percent for industrial countries and one percent for the non-oil developing countries over the same period. A significant explanation may lie in the expansion of agriculture and petrochemicals in the 1970s both of which are energy-intensive.

Because of the rapid rise in real oil prices in recent years, the cost of primary energy has risen considerably relative to the general price level. Government policy was to pass the rise on to consumers. The structure of final energy prices is influenced by the operation of the Equalization fund. This collects tax on some petroleum products, mainly gasoline and liquid petroleum gas, and subsidizes others, mainly diesel oil, fuel oil and naphtha.

Israeli Energy Imports
(thousands of tons)

	1972	1974	1978	1980	1981	1982
Crude oil	6,291	6,908	7,975	7,399	6,887	8,266
Petroleum Products	57	49	204	1,561	1,571	330
Coal	—	—	—	—	361	990
Total Hydrocarbons	6,348	6,957	8,179	8,960	8,819	9,586

Israeli Energy Imports
(millions of U.S. $)

Total oil	98	598	775	2,116	2,043	1,914
Of which: Crude Oil	93	584	762	1,799	1,685	1,790

9.2 REDUCING DEPENDENCE. For obvious security reasons, Israel is making strenuous efforts to decrease its dependence on imported oil. Solar energy production, for which Israel is geographically well qualified, is receiving considerable attention and an experiemental pilot plan is in operation. A canal to drop water from the Mediterranean to the Dead Sea to produce hydroelectricity has been under discussion since the 1940s; the idea has recently been revived but may produce as many problems as solutions. Also, in an effort to decrease dependence on oil, Israel is switching to coal — also an import — to fuel thermal electricity plants.

10.
PUBLIC FINANCE

10.1 REVENUE. Budget revenues have increased substantially in relation to GNP, while both tax revenue, which is
70-80 percent of total revenue, and non-tax revenue went
up sharply. In 1975 a reform of income tax was introduced
which extended the tax base from 1975 to the end of 1979,
income tax brackets were only partly updated. They were
adjusted once every six months to 70 percent of the rise
in the consumer price index. Mounting inflation, however,
eroded the brackets, leading to higher tax receipts and
demand for pay increases. Since 1980, tax bracket
adjustments have been fully linked to the rise in the
consumer price index; since 1981 adjustments have been
made every three months.

The prolonged rapid inflation has exposed defects in
the tax collection and income redistribution machinery. A
comparison of company income tax receipts with government
payments to the business sector (under the law for the
encouragement of capital investments through direct
credits and other concessions) reveals that the net amount
left for financing other government activities is small
and perhaps even negative.

Among indirect taxes the most important is the value
added tax (VAT), which is a tax on sales. Introduced in
1976, VAT quickly became the principal indirect tax on
domestic production. It accounted recently for almost one
fifth of total government revenues.

While income taxation is progressive, and subsidies
are available to low-income families, the sales tax and
the government's growing dependence on the inflationary
process to appropriate resources for public use implies
that the poor, who spend a larger proportion of their
income on consumption, are severely penalized.

10.2 GOVERNMENT EXPENDITURES. Government expenditures
have grown substantially in relation to GNP, from about 68
percent in the late 1970s to nearly 100 percent in 1983.
A large part of the increase in current spending has been

Government Revenue
(in billions of Shekels)

	1978/79	1979/80	1980/81	1981/82	1982/83
Total Revenue	12.5	26.3	66.7	142.7	365.5
Tax Revenue	10.2	20.9	46.0	106.6	299.1
Taxes on Income,					
Profit, Gains	4.6	10.1	23.7	53.9	148.3
Individuals	2.9	7.0	17.8	25.0	--
Corporates	1.2	2.7	5.5	11.1	--
Other	0.5	0.4	0.4	7.8	--
Payroll Taxes	0.5	1.1	3.3	7.8	19.0
Property Taxes	0.2	0.5	0.8	2.0	3.3
Domestic Taxes on	3.6	6.7	14.3	34.7	107.0
Goods, Services					
VAT	3.2	5.7	12.5	20.2	73.4
Excises	0.4	0.8	1.6	9.9	22.7
Other	-	0.2	0.2	4.6	10.9
Import Duties	0.6	1.1	2.1	5.5	21.5
Other Taxes	0.7	1.4	1.8	2.7	--
Non-tax Revenue	2.2	5.4	20.7	36.1	66.5
Income from					
Enterprises	0.8	2.2	7.9	13.5	18.1
Interest Income	0.4	0.9	1.5	4.5	7.2
Profits from Bank					
of Israel	0.3	1.1	5.3	4.9	14.0
Other	0.8	1.2	6.0	13.2	27.2

in defense-related activity. Defense expenditures account for about a quarter of GNP. Even if U.S. government aid is excluded, the weight of such outlays financed by the domestic economy is high in comparison with those of other western countries. The defense burden and the large energy bill since 1973 are among the factors responsible for the inflationary spiral.

Expenditures on social and welfare services and subsidies, secured by indexation, have risen rapidly. There are large subsidies on bread, on public transportation, and on other commodities of mass consumption. Subsidies are paid by the government to the public in two forms: public subsidies, paid through the National Institute of Social Security, are based solely on family size, while indirect subsidies are paid to reduce the cost of staples and mass transportation to the consumer. Austerity measures will reduce both especially the latter.

Welfare legislation in the mid-1970s and more recently in 1980/81 has aimed at preserving or icreasing social benefits and allowances in real terms, the establishment of new educational institutions, and an expansion in social health services. These intitiatives entailed an expansion in public employment at a time when other policies were attempting to restructure employment away from public services and towards the traded goods sector. There is a long-term rising trend in the weight of employment: at the beginning of the 1960s, one fifth of all employed in the economy were in public services; in the first half of the 1970s the proportion rose to a fourth, and in current years it reached 30 percent. The expansion of public civilian services and the high level of defense spending are not consistent with the principal economic targets of Israel: the renewal of growth, reduction of balance of the payments deficit, and the mastering of inflation.

Finally, interest payments on the growing public debt have accelerated; their weight in total expenditure is now about 16 percent.

10.3 ECONOMIC DECISION-MAKING. The Ministry of Finance plays the major role in Israeli economic life. Other economic ministries, like the ministries of Industry and Trade, Energy and Infrastructure, Construction and Housing, and Transport have little influence on the process of macro-economic decision making. The planning authority, a subordinate of the Finance Ministry plays a minor role in that process.

A subject of debate in Israel is whether the Bank of Israel (the central bank) should be an independent entity or should only serve to implement the policy of the Finance Ministry. In fact, the bank operates under severe constraints, most of them imposed by the Ministry of Finance, and the economic policy tools at its disposal are ineffective.

11.
FINANCIAL SECTOR

11.1 OVERVIEW. Israeli financial institutions comprise: commercial banks, banks for the development of an economic sector (industry, agriculture), mortgage banks, investment companies, and households finance companies. Also included in the financial sector are primary financial intermediaries such as social insurance funds, insurance companies and mutual funds. In line with accelerating inflation, the size and domestic activity of the financial sector have grown substantially. There are three major commercial banks in Israel: Bank Leumi Le Israel, Hapoalim Bank and Israeli Discount Bank, which hold more than four-fifths of public deposits. These banks oversee some of the investment and insurance companies, meeting most of their capital requirements through the flotation of stock issues on the stock market.

11.2 GOVERNMENT INFLUENCE ON FINANCIAL SECTOR ACTIVITY. Government involvement is discernible throughout the entire process of financial intermediation. In mobilizing "primary" resources (mainly from households, through social insurance, pension funds, insurance companies, savings schemes, and trust funds), the government ensures that the lion's share of voluntary saving finds its way into the financial system by guaranteeing public savings directly or indirectly. At the intermediate stage the government insures through regulation that most resources are channeled to the acquisition of bonds, government-issued as well as those of financial institutions. Finally, financial means are placed at the disposal of the various economic sectors and households (small businesses and selected consumers) to finance their activities as producers and consumers through payment of subsidies.

11.3 THE BANK OF ISRAEL. Bank of Israel is responsible for formulation and implementation of monetary policy. The Bank has at least six classes of policy instruments at its disposal:

- Open market operation. By selling bonds to the public, the Bank of Israel causes bank reserves (the monetary base and eventually the money supply) to contract; a purchase of government bonds has the opposite effect.
- Manipulation of the "discount rate" through variation in the fines paid on liquidity deficiencies by the banks. A higher discount rate at the Bank of Israel reduces free reserves held by banks and causes the money supply to contract.
- Credit ceilings imposed on banking system, in particular limits on credit to the private sector.
- Foreign exchange market intervention, entailing buying and selling foreign exchange.
- Control over borrowing rates from abroad.
- Other administrative measures.

Bank of Israel Balance Sheet
(Millions of Shekels)

	12/31/81	12/31/82
Assets		
Foreign Assets	55,376	136,417
Government Debt	24,546	81,337
Loans and Discounts	22,330	18,355
Securities	9,558	22,044
Other Accounts	3,154	5,634
Total	114,964	263,787
Liabilities		
Bank Notes and Coins in Circulation	5,360	10,722
Foreign Liabilities	1,417	1,501
Allocation of S.D.R's	1,928	3,960
Foreign Currency Deposits of Government	4,281	14,866
Foreign Currency Deposits of Banking Institutions	86,042	198,799
Deposits of Banking and Financial Institutions	4,424	12,687
Other Accounts	11,512	21,252
Total	114,964	263,787

The Bank operates within a number of significant constraints. It is given very little leeway in setting the prices of new issues of government bonds; the subsidized credit for exports given by the Bank constitutes a large part of the credit supplied to the domestic economy. The bank is constrained by the need to maintain the financial viability of the banking system. And above all there is often a lack of coordination between the government and the Bank. Many of the most important questions about monetary policy in Israel concern appropriate Bank responses to anticipated government actions with financial ramifications.

11.4 FINANCIAL MARKETS. Israeli financial markets differ from those of the western countries in three major respects:

- There is substantial government involvement in market activity throughout the entire process of financial mediation.
- The weight of commercial bank shares among the stock exchange securities is high. The banks have been supporting their stock by active intervention in market activity. This intervention has led the investing public to expect their shares to be quite liquid and to yield a high return; demand has shifted from other financial assets to these securities. For a period of time, this phenomonem encouraged many Israelies to engage in speculation on a full-time basis.
- In line with the increasing inflation rate, the share of liquid assets in the financial assets of the public has been shrinking; at the end of 1982, it stood at a mere 2 percent.

IV. ISRAEL: STATISTICAL APPENDIX[*]

---

[*] Statistics included in this section do not include data for the Occupied Territories.

Table 1.

BASIC INFORMATION

Official name: Medinat Israel — State of Israel

Date of Independence: May 14, 1948

National Flag: White with 2 horizontal blue stripes, the blue Shield of David in the center.

National Anthem Title: Hatikvah (The Hope)

Weights and Measures: The metric system is in general use. The (metrical) dunam = 1,000 sq m (about 0.25 acres)

Time: GMT + 3

Currency units: Shekel= 10 Israeli pounds.

Languages: Hebrew, Arabic, Yiddish

Area: 21,501 sq km, the "Green Line" border before the 1967 war includes East Jerusalem.

Bodies of water: Dead Sea, Sea of Galilee (Lake Tiberias, Lake Kinneret)

Capital City: Jerusalem — Proclaimed by Israel as the capital Aug. 31, 1980 but not recognized diplomatically.

Population: 4.06 million (83% Jewish)

Nature of Government: Parliamentary democracy

Date of Constitution: There is no formal Constitution. The Transition Law deals with the powers of the Knesset, President and Cabinet. The Knesset enacts fundamental laws, which eventually will comprise the Constitution (along with the Transition Law).

Foreign Policy Position: Pro-Western

Diplomatic Representatives:

    U.S. ambassador: Samuel Lewis
    Ambasador to U.S.: Meir Rosenne
    Ambassador to U.N.: Yehuda Blum

Past Presidents:

Chaim Weizmann (1949-52)	Ephraim Katzir (1963-78)
Izhak Ben-Zvi (1952-63)	Yitzhak Navon (1978-1983)
Zalman Shazar (1963-68)	Chaim Herzog (1983-present)

Table 2.

GOVERNMENT OF ISRAEL

Position	Name	Party Affiliation
President	Chaim Herzog	Labor
Prime Minister	Shimon Peres	Labor
Deputy Prime Minister & Foreign Minister	Yitzhak Shamir	Likud
Agriculture	Arieh Nehamkin	Labor
Communications	Amnon Rubinstein	Shinui
Defense	Yitzhak Rabin	Labor
Economy & Planning	Gad Yaakobi	Labor
Education & Culture	Yitzhak Navon	Labor
Energy & Infrastructure	Moshe Shehel	Labor
Finance	Yitzhak Modai	Likud-Liberal
Health	Mordechai Gur	Labor
Interior	Shimon Peres	Labor
Justice	Moshe Nissim	Likud-Liberal
Labor & Social Welfare	Moshe Katsav	Likud-Herut
Immigrant Absorption	Yaacov Taur	Labor
Police	Haim Bar-Lev	Labor
Religious Affairs	Shimon Peres	Labor
Science & Development	Gideon Pat	Likud-Liberal
Tourism	Avraham Sharir	Likud
Trade & Industry	Ariel Sharon	Likud-Herut
Transportation	Haim Corfu	Likud-Herut
Minister in the Prime Minister's Cabinet	Ezer Weitzmann	Labor

Ministers Without Portfolio

	Moshe Arens	Likud-Herut
	Yosef Burg	NRP
	Yigal Horowitz	Ometz
	Yitzhak Peretz	Shas
	Yosef Shapira	Morasha

[Cabinet formed September 13, 1984]

Past Prime Ministers:

David Ben-Gurion (1948-1953)	Golda Meir (1969-1974)
Moshe Sharett (1953-1955)	Yitzhak Rabin (1974-1977)
David Ben-Gurion (1955-1963)	Menachem Begin (1977-1983)
Levi Eshkol (1963-1969)	Yitzhak Shamir (1983-present)

Table 3.

POLITICAL PARTIES IN ISRAEL

Orientation	Name	Platform	Leadership
Communist	Hadash-Rakah	Pro-Arab splinter of former communist party; supports return to 1967 borders and Palestinian state	Meir Vilner Tufik Tubi
Left-wing	Progressive List for Peace	A largely Arab party with some former Shelli members Supports creation of Palestinian state and negotiations with PLO.	Matti Peled Muhamed Meari
Socialist	Labor (Labor & Mapam)	Moderate socialist; supports socialist economy, welfare state, territorial compromise, Palestinian -Jordanian federation	Shimon Peres Yitzhak Rabin Victor Shem-Tov Yitzhak Navon
Center	Shinui	Supports free economy, territorial compromise	Amnon Rubinstein
Center	Civil Rights Movement	Defense of civil rights in Israel and occupied territorial compromise establishing Palestinian entity	Shulamit Aloni
Center	Yahad	Supports free economy and territorial compromise	Ezer Weitzmann Benjamin Ben Aliezer
Center	Onetz	Party dedicated to restructuring the economy	Yigal Horowitz
Ethnic	Tami	Supports political power for Sephardim; close to Likud in foreign policy.	Aharon Abuhatzeir Aharon Uzan

POLITICAL PARTIES IN ISRAEL

ientation	Name	Platform	Leadership
ght-wing	Likud (Liberal & Herut)	Supports mixed free economy with welfare measures to protect weak socio-economic groups; favors de facto annexation of West Bank, opposes creation of Palestinian entity	Yitzhak Shamir David Levy Ariel Sharon Moshe Shamir Gideon Pat Yitzhak Mudai
ght-wing	Tehiya	Ultra-right splinter from Herut; advocates annexation of West Bank, permanent Israeli presence in Lebanon	Geula Cohen Yuval Ne'eman Moshe Shamir
ght-wing	Kach	Ultra-right party; supports annexation of West Bank, deportation of Palestinians	Meir Kahane
ligious	National Religious Party	Moderately religious; supports moderate socialist economy, religious legislation, Jewish sovereignty over West Bank	Yosef Burg
ligious	Agudat Israel	Ultra-orthodox religious; advocates Jewish state based on halacha (religious law), supports Jewish settlements on West Bank	Avraham Shapira Shlomo Lorincz
ligious	Shas: Sephardi Guardians of the Torah	Ultra-orthodox Sephardi splinter from Agudat Israel; Supports a halacha state and annexation of West Bank	Yitzhak Peretz Raphael Pinhasi
ligious	Morasha	A national-religious party backed by the Gush Emunim; advocates annexation of West Bank	Haim Drukmann Abraham Varoliger Hanan Porat

DEFENSE

122

Table 4.

MILITARY EQUIPMENT AND PERSONNEL

Chief of Staff of the Armed Forces: Moshe Levi
Head of Ground Forces Command: Major-General Israel Tal
Commander of the Air Force: Major-General David Ivri
Comander of the Navy: Commodore Zeev Almog

Type of Military Service: Men — 39 months, Women— 24 months (Jews an Druze only; Christians may volunteer). Annual training for reserves thereafter up to age 54 for men, 34 (or marriage) for women.

Total armed forces: 172,000 (120,300 conscripts); mobilization to 500,000, of which 100,000 can be mobilized in about 24 hours

Estimated defense expenditure 1982: IS 200.0 bn ($8.242 bn).
                       1983: IS 280.0 bn ($6.461 bn).

Army: 135,000 (110,000 conscripts, male and female)
           450,000 on mobilization, incl civil defence units.

11 armored divisions
33 armored brigades (3 tank, 1 mechanized infantry battalions)
10 mechanized infantry brigades (5 para-trained)
12 territorial/border infantry brigades with Nahal militia
15 artillery brigades (each 5 batallions of 3 batteries)

Armoured fighting vehicles: 3,600 tanks, including 1,100 Centurion, 650 M-48, 1,010 M-60, 440 T-54/-55, 150 T-62, 250 Merkava I/II; about 4,000 armoured reconnaissance vehicles incl RBY RAM, BRDM-1/-2, Shoet Mk 2 M-2/-3, 4,000 M-113, OT-62, BTR-40/-50P/-60P/-152, Walid APC.

Artillery: 130mm, 140 M-107 175mm SP guns; 70 M-101 105mm, 100 122mm, M-68/-71 155mm towed, 300 155mm L-33 and M-50, Soltam M-72, 300 M-109 155mm, 48 M-110 203mm SP how; 122mm, 135mm, 240mm, 290mm, MRL; Lance SSM; 900 81mm, 120mm and 160mm mor (some self-propelled).

Anti-tank: B-300 Ze'ev (Wolf), 82mm RL; 106mm RCL; TOW, Cobra, Dragon Picket, Milan guided weapons.

Anti-aircraft: 2 batteries with 24 Vulcan/Chaparral 20mm gun/ms. systems, 900 20mm, 30mm, and 40mm anti-aircraft guns; Redeye SAM.

(On order: 125 M-60 tanks; Re'em armoured fighting vehicles; 800 M-113 amoured personnel carriers; 200 M-109A1B self-propelled 155mm howitzers M-107 175mm SP guns; Lance SSM; TOW, Dragon anti-tank guided weapon.)

Source: Military Balance, 1983

Navy: 9,000 (3,300 conscripts), 10,000 on mobilization

3 Type 206 submarines
2 Aliya (Saar 4.5) corvettes with 4 Gabriel, 2 Harpoon SSM, 1 Bell 206
    anti-submarine helicopters.
20 Fast attack craft(M): 8 Reshef (Saar 4) with 5 Gabriel and 4 Harpoon
    SSM; 6 Saar 2 with 6 Gabriel, 6 Saar 3 with 5-8 Gabriel.
2 Flagstaff 2 hydrofoil FAC(M) with 2 Gabriel, 2 Harpoon SSM
45 coastal patrol craft: 37 Dabur, 2 Dvora, 6 Hawk.
1 Landing ship, tank; 3 US landing ship, missiles; 3 utility landing
    craft
4 Seascan 1124N maritime reconnaissance aircraft (mrac)
Naval commando: (300)
(On order: 4 Saar 5 corvettes, 3 Seascan mrac.)

Bases: Haifa, Ashdod, Eilat

Air Force: 28,000 (2,000 conscripts, mostly in AD)
                37,000 on mobilization
550 combat aircrat (90 in store)
42 combat helicopters
5 fighters, ground attack/interceptor sqadrons: 2 with 40 F/TF-15;
    5 with 131 F-4E; 5 with 150 Kfir-C1/C2; 3 with 64 F-16A, 8 F-16B.
4 fighter ground attack squadrons with 130 A-4N/J Skyhawk.
    Reconnaissnace: 13 RF-4E, 2 OV-1E; 4 E-2C Airborn early warning;
    4 RU-21J, 2 C-130, 4 Boeing 707 electronic counter-measure aircraft.
1 transport wing: incl 7 Boeing 707 (2 tanker mods), 20 C-130E/H,
    18 C-47, 2 KC-130H.
Liaison: 1 Islander, 5 Do-27, 14 Do-28D; 18 Cessna U-206C, 2 T-41D, 2
    180; 12 Queen Air 80; 2 Westwind; 20 Super Cub.
Trainers: 73 TA-4E/H, 50 Kfir (incl TC-2), 85 Magister/Amit.
Helicpoters: 8 Super Frelon, 33 CH-53D, 12 AH-1G/S, 2 S-65C, 25 Bell 206,
    60 Bell 212, 17 UH-1D, 30 Hughes 500MD hel.
Drones: Mastiff 2, Scout, Teledyne Ryan 124R.
15 SAM batallions with Improved HAWK.
Air-to-air missiles: Sidewinder, AIM-7E/F Sparrow, Shafrir, Python III,
    Gabriel III (mod).
Air-to-surface missiles: Luz, Maverick, Shrike, Walleye, Bullpup.

(On order: 11 F-15, 72 F-16 fighters, Lavi fighters, 60 Kfir TC-2
training aircraft; 200 Improved HAWK SAM; 200 Sidewinder AAM.)

Reserves: (all services): 326,000.
Forces Abroad: Lebanon (20,000).

Para-Military Forces: Border Guards 4,500; BTR-152 Armoured personnel
carrier. Arab Militia: small arms.
Coastguard: 3 ex-US PBR, 3 other patrol craft.

Table 5.

ISRAELI MILITARY EXPENDITURE 1972-1982
(constant 1981 dollars)

Year	Military Expenditure (billion U.S. $)	% of GNP	% of Central Govt. Expenditure
1972	2.87	17.6	39.8
1973	5.78	34.1	54.8
1974	5.14	28.6	43.3
1975	5.86	31.9	43.3
1976	5.99	32.7	41.0
1977	5.69	30.0	34.8
1978	4.78	24.3	34.0
1979	6.23	30.8	38.6
1980	5.93	29.3	34.2
1981	4.37*	20.3	20.0
1982	5.50*	25.5	28.7

*Estimated

Source: U.S. Arms Control and Disarmament Agency

Table 6.

ISRAELI MILITARY EXPENDITURE AS % OF GDP

1975	25.6
1976	26.7
1977	27.4
1978	25.4
1979	20.7
1980	13.8
1981	19.1

Source: SIPRI Yearbook, 1983

Table 7.

ISRAELI ARMS IMPORTS AND EXPORTS
(million U.S. $) /1

Year	Arms Imports Current Prices	Arms Imports Constant 1981 $	% Total Imports	Arms Exports Current Prices	Arms Exports Constant 1981 $	% Total Exports
1972	300	583	12.1	10	19	0.9
1973	230	421	5.3	20	36	1.4
1974	950	1608	17.4	30	50	1.6
1975	725	1125	11.8	50	77	2.6
1976	975	1432	17.0	140	205	5.8
1977	1100	1526	19.0	60	83	1.9
1978	900	1162	11.9	120	155	3.1
1979	490	583	5.6	260	309	5.7
1980	825	901	8.4	140	153	2.5
1981	1100	1100	10.7	260	260	4.6
1982	1000	943	10.3	360	339	6.9

/1 Country imports are reported cif and country exports fob.

Source: World Military Expenditures and Arms Transfers
U.S. Arms Control and Disarmament Agency, 1984

Table 8.

VALUE OF ARMS TRANSFERS BY MAJOR SUPPLIERS
(cumulative 1978-1982 million current U.S. $)

Total	4,415
United States	4,400
Italy	10
Other	5

Source: World Military Expenditures and Arms Transfers
U.S. Arms Control and Disarmament Agency, 1984

Table 9.

TRADE IN MAJOR CONVENTIONAL WEAPONS

Supplier	No. Ordered	Weapon ----Description--------		Year Ordered	Year Delivered	No. Ordered
USA	600	AGM-65A	ASM	1979	1980	250
	40	F-15A Eagle	Fighter/ Interceptor	1978	1978 1979 1980 1981 1982	3 5 5 17 10
	11	F-15A	Fighter/ Interceptor	1982		
	75	F-16A	Fighter/ Striker	1982		
	1	Flagstaff-2	Hydrofoil FAC	1977	1982	1
	200	M-109 A1 155mm	SPH	1979	1980 1981 1982	50 50 50

APC=Armoured personnel carrier   FAC=Fast attack craft
ARV=Armoured recovery vehicle   MBT=Main battle tank
ASM=Air-to-surface missile   SAM=Surface-to-air missile
ATM=Anti-tank missile   ShShM=Ship to ship missile
CPC=Command post carrier   SPH=Self-propelled howitzer

Source: SIPRI Yearbook, 1983

TRADE IN MAJOR CONVENTIONAL WEAPONS

Supplier	No. Ordered	Weapon ----Description--------		Year Ordered	Year Delivered	No. Ordered
SA	56	M548	APC	1979	1981	20
					1982	36
	98	M577-A1	CPC	1979	1981	50
					1982	48
	300	M60-A3	MBT	1979	1980	50
					1981	50
					1982	65
	25	M-88-A1	ARV	1979	1981	11
					1982	14
	200	MIM-23B Hawk	Landmob SAM	1982		
	250	Chaparral	Landmob SAM	1979		
	18	Model 209 AH-IS	Helicopter	1981		
	100	RGM-84A	ShshM	1979	1980	25
					1981	25
					1982	25

Table 10.

MAJOR ISRAELI ARMS SALES TO LATIN AMERICA 1970-1980

Country	Arms Deliveries
Argentina	26 Dassault Mirage Fighters 22 Nesher Eagle Fighters 50 Gabriel Missiles Shafrir Missiles
Bolivia	6 Arava (STOL) Transports
Chile	150 Shafrir Missilis 1 Radar System 2 Reshef Class Fast Patrol Boats
Colombia	3 Araba (STOL) Transports
Dominican Republic	9-mm Uzi Submachine Guns
Ecuador	10 Arava (STOL) Transports Ammunition Rockets Explosives
El Salvador	17 Arava (STOL) Transports 6 Fouga Magister Trainers 18 Dassault Ouragan Fighters 200 80-mm Rocket Launchers 200 9-mm Uzi Submachine Guns Ammunition Spare Parts
Guatemala	11 Arava (STOL) Transports 10 RBY Mk Armored Cars 15,000 5.56-mm Galil Assault Rifles 4 Field Kitchens

Source: American-Arab Anti-Discrimination Committee, Paper #8

MAJOR ISRAELI ARMS SALES TO LATIN AMERICA 1970-1980

Country	Arms Deliveries
Haiti	600 9-mm Uzi Submachine Guns 106-mm Rifles
Honduras	12 Dassault Super Mystere Fighters 4 Arava (STOL) Transports 1 Westwind Reconnaissance Plane 106-mm Mortars 14 RBY Mk Armored Cars 106-mm Rifles 5 Fast Patrol Boats (unconfirmed)
Mexico	10 Arava (STOL) Transports
Nicaragua	2 Arava (STOL) Transports Rifles Ammunitions Patrol Boats Radios
Panama	1 Westwind Reconnaissance Plane
Paraguay	6 Arava (STOL) Transports
Peru	Parachutes Radio Equipment Ammunition Small Arms
Venezuela	Bombs Rockets Tactical Communications Equipment

Table 11.
FOREIGN INVESTMENT IN ISRAEL'S MILITARY INDUSTRIES

Corporation	Israeli Subsidiary (date founded)	% Owned	Products
Aarhus Chefabrik	Hayes (Ashdod) Ltd.	na	na
American Electronic Laboratories (AEL)	AEL Israel Ltd. (1967)	37	Avionics, military electronics
Astronautics Corp. America Ltd.	Astronautics C.A. Ltd. (1970)	100	Avionics, generators, etc.
Control Data Corporation	Eljim Ltd.	100	Military computers
	Eltek Ltd.	67	na
	Elbit Computers Ltd. (1966)	37	Electronic warfare equipment
	Contahal Israel	50	na
	World Technologies Israel Ltd.		na
	Control Data Israel	100	na
	Elron	na	na
Austin Instruments Inc. (NY)	Precision Mechanism Ltd.		Electronics, mechanical goods
Chromalloy America	Turbochrome		Engine turbines
Designatronics Inc.	Automatic Coil of Israel Ltd.	na	Electronics, mechanical component
Digital Equipment Corp.	DECSYS Computers Ltd.	100	Military computer parts
General Telephone & Electronics	Tadiran Israel Electronics Ind.	45	Military electroni computers, communi cations equipment
	Advanced Technologies Ltd.	na	na
Gerber Scientific Inc.	Beta Engineering & Development Ltd.	54	Anti-guerilla detection systems, mine detection devices
Intel Corporation	Intel Israel	100	Electronic computers, computer circuits
Information Magnetic Corp.	SDSI Scientific Data Systems Israel	na	na

Source: MERIP Report, February 1983

tek Corporation	Sci-Tex Corp.	na	Optical systems
MS Industries Inc.	KMS	na	Military avionics, computers
Kulicke & Soffa Industries Inc.	Kulso Ltd. Monsel Electronics Industries Ltd.	na na	na na
Landseas Corp. (NYC)	Landseas Israel (1962)	na	Electronics, computers
Locke Technology Inc.	Laser Industries	na	na
Mennen Greatbach Electronics	Mennen Electronics	na	na
Metal Working Laser International	Metal Working Laser, Ltd.	na	Computer welding machinery
Microwave Associates	Science-Based Ind. (Technion)	na	na
Motorola Inc.	Motorola Israel	100	Military communications systems
Neuchatel Suisse Holding Financiere Industriele	Israelelectra, Ltd.	na	computers, military electronics
Pioneer Systems Inc.	Pioneer Enterprises (Aerodyne), Ltd.	na	na
Rand Information Systems	Arand Iltam		Computers Computers
Teledyne Inc.	Teledyne Intercontinental, Ltd.	na	Electronic control systems
Turbomecha	Ormat Turbines, Ltd.	na	na
TRW	Iscan Blades	na	Spares for Mirage, Phantom, Kfir; engine parts
VALTEC	Fibronics Communications Equipment		na
Veeco Instruments	Islambda Electronics	100	na
Vishay Intertechnology	Vishay Israel (1969)	100	na
Whittaker Corp.	Orlite Engineering		Ttrucks and aircraft

Table 12

UNITED STATES MILITARY ASSISTANCE TO ISRAEL
(mn $)

| | Total U.S. Aid to Israel | Military Loans | Military Grants | Economic Aid | |
				Loans	Grants
1977	1,757	500.0	500.0	252.0	490.0
1978	1,812	500.0	500.0	266.8	525.0
1979	4,815	2,700.0	1,300.0	265.1	525.0
1980	1,811	500.0	500.0	261.0	525.0
1981	2,189	900.0	500.0	--	764.0
1982	2,219	850.0	550.0	--	806.3
1983 /1	2,198	850.0	550.0	--	785.0

/1 Under the Continuing Appropriations Act, 1983 which expired Dec. 17, 1982.

Source: Library of Congress Congressional Research Service

ECONOMY

134

Table 13.

GROSS DOMESTIC PRODUCT BY SECTOR
(current factor cost mn of shekels)

	1977	1978	1979	1980	1981
Agriculture	776.1	1179.0	2173.0	5201.0	11830.0
Manufacturing	3137.0	5959.0	10308.0	23220.0	59714.0
Construction	1220.9	1576.0	3586.0	9585.0	22279.0
Transport and Communications	990.4	1574.0	2737.0	6107.0	15180.0
Trade and Public Finance	3328.1	2666.0	4999.0	11077.0	26316.0
Public Administration	2632.6	---	---	---	---
Other	346.8	7514.5	16695.0	39236.3	98870.0

Source: World Bank Economic Data, 1983

Table 14.

NET DOMESTIC PRODUCT AT FACTOR COST BY SECTOR
(IS mn)

	1978	1979	1980	1981	1982
Agriculture	1,174	2,173	5,358	12,109	27,062
Industry /1	4,293	7,114	16,969	39,471	86,965
Construction /2	1,942	4,110	10,051	21,694	46,386
Commerce	2,534	4,775	10,589	25,091	59,802
Transport, Storage and Communications	1,482	2,591	5,648	14,575	30,341
Finance and Business Services	2,634	5,506	13,304	29,872	67,390
Personal and Other Services	607	1,097	2,349	5,507	13,593
Net Domestic Product	20,428	40,006	90,962	211,972	466,591
Gross National Product (at market prices)	23,222	43,844	102,198	243,067	538,952

/1 includes mining
/2 includes electricity and water

Source: Statistical Abstract of Israel, 1983

Table 15.

EXCHANGE RATES 1977-1983
(shekels per U.S. Dollar)

1976	0.794
1977	1.046
1978	1.746
1979	2.544
1980	5.124
1981	11.431
1982	24.267
1983	56.214

Source: IMF International Financial Statistics, 1984

Table 16.

CONSUMER PRICE INDEX
(annual average)

Base: 1959=100.0

1960	102.9
1962	120.2
1964	134.7

Base: 1964=100.0

1966	116.3
1968	120.7

Base: 1969=100.0

1970	106.1
1972	134.1
1974	224.8
1976	411.2

Base: 1976=100.0

1978	202.7
1979	361.4
1980	834.9

Base: 1980=100.0

1981	216.8
1982	477.7
1983 April	934.9

Annual growth rate of inflation (consumer price index 1981): 101.5%

Source: Statistical Abstract of Israel 1983

Table 17.

FINANCIAL SURVEY

	1978	1979	1980	1981

International Liquidity
(mn $ unless otherwise indicated)

	1978	1979	1980	1981
Foreign Exchange Reserves	2,597.8	3,015.6	3,307.5	3,496.0
Gold (mn fine troy ounces)	1.171	1.231	1.194	1.193
Gold (national valuation)	53.4	56.8	53.3	48.6
SDRs	27.3	6.3	11.2	0.7
Reserve Position in Fund	---	41.6	32.7	---

Deposit Money Banks
(IS bn)

	1978	1979	1980	1981
Claims on Government	1.6	4.6	14.0	37.9
Claims on Private Sector	13.5	29.4	69.9	154.7
Foreign Assets	6.6	15.3	41.7	97.8
Reserves	1.1	1.1	2.4	5.4
Foreign Liabilities	8.9	21.9	57.3	142.7
Demand Deposits	1.8	2.3	4.9	8.1
Time and Saving Deposits	16.3	35.4	84.7	189.3

Bank of Israel
(IS bn)

	1978	1979	1980	1981
Foreign Assets	5.6	11.2	26.3	55.4
Claims on Government	3.5	5.7	9.0	34.1
Claims on Deposit Money Banks	3.3	8.0	19.3	27.4
Reserves	2.0	2.3	4.5	9.8
Foreign Liabilities	0.7	1.1	1.6	1.9
Government deposits	0.6	1.0	2.3	4.3
Other	9.1	20.4	46.4	100.9

Monetary Survey
(IS bn)

	1978	1979	1980	1981
Money	2.7	3.5	7.0	12.5
Quasi Money	16.3	35.4	84.7	189.3
Other	0.9	1.6	4.3	17.4

Source: International Financial Statistics Yearbook, 1984

FINANCIAL SURVEY

	1982	1983
International Liquidity (mn $ unless otherwise indicated)		
Foreign exchange reserves	3,838.7	3,613.1
Gold (mn fine troy ounces)	1.084	1.015
Gold (national valuation)	41.9	37.2
SDRs	0.6	1.7
Reserve position in Fund	---	36.4
Deposit Money Banks (IS bn)		
Claims on government	114.5	389.7
Claims on private sector	370.0	969.8
Foreign Assets	238.4	737.7
Reserves	10.2	24.5
Foreign Liabilities	378.4	1,170.1
Demand Deposits	17.8	37.6
Time and saving deposits	469.4	1,447.1
Bank of Israel (IS bn)		
Foreign Assets	136.4	409.8
Claims on Government	103.4	493.7
Claims on Deposit Money Banks	18.4	82.6
Reserves	23.4	52.5
Foreign Liabilities	1.5	1.5
Government deposits	14.9	86.5
Other	218.4	845.6
Monetary Survey (IS bn)		
Money	26.8	64.7
Quasi Money	469.4	1,447.1
Other	40.8	107.9

Table 18.

CREDIT BY BANKING INSTITUTIONS, BY ECONOMIC DESTINATION
(IS million, at current prices; end of year)

	1981	1982
Total	**168,403**	**419,540**
Local Authorities	12,208	29,691
Public Services	4,636	10,917
Electricity and Water	8,379	18,253
Financial Institutions	21,053	57,547
The Jewish Agency and the National Fund	717	1,134
Agriculture	16,373	42,952
Industry	43,064	97,179
Building	4,768	14,246
Commerce	24,092	51,628
Transport	10,878	25,785
Other Services	3,105	9,625
Private Persons	7,262	34,069
Foreign Residents	11,323	22,989
Other Destinations and Not Known	545	3,526

Source: Statistical Abstract of Israel, 1983

Table 19.

STOCK MARKET VALUATION BY SECTOR
(mn $)

	12/83	4/84	% Change
Commercial Banks	3,096,078	3,874,038	25.13
Mortgage Banks	265,397	176,672	-33.43
Financial Institutions	104,894	221,719	13.76
Insurance Firms	107,178	77,326	-27.85
Commercial Services	133,045	166,776	26.10
Real Estate and Property Development	733,759	229,706	- 1.73
Industrial Companies	819,374	772,076	- 5.77
Investment Companies	475,284	431,026	- 9.61
Oil Search Firms	42,375	53,564	26.33
Total	**5,367,390**	**5,999,871**	**11.78**

Source: Israeli Economist, May 1984

DEMOGRAPHY

Table 20.

CHIEF DEMOGRAPHIC INDICATORS
(1982)

Population, Total (in thousands)	4,063.6
Population, Male (in thousands)	2,028.9
Population, Female (in thousands)	2,034.7
Population Ages (% of total):	
0-4	11.6
5-14	21.8
15-19	8.6
20-24	8.2
25-34	15.9
35-44	10.1
44-64	15.5
65+	8.4
Median Age:	
Total	24.4
Male	23.6
Female	25.2
Average Size of Household	3.64
Divorce Rate (per 1000)	1.2
Urban Population (% of total, 1981)	86.8
Birth Rate (live births per 1000)	24.0
Death Rate (per 1000)	6.9
Net Reproduction Rate	1.48
Gross Reproduction Rate	1.51
General Fertility Rate	102.7
Life Expectancy:	
Male	75.8
Female	72.5

Source: UN Demographic Yearbook, Statistical Abstract of Israel, 1983

Table 21.

POPULATION OF MAJOR CITIES (1981)

Major Cities	Population
Beer Sheva	111,200
Bat Yam	132,800
Holon	132,300
Haifa	227,400
Jerusalem	415,000
Petah Tiqva	121,700
Ramat Gan	119,100
Tel Aviv-Yafo	329,500

Source: Statistical Abstract of Israel, 1983

Table 22.

POPULATION BY POPULATION GROUP, ORIGIN, CONTINENT OF BIRTH AND RELIGION (1982)

Total	4,063,600
Jews – Total	3,373,200
Origin: Israel	532,800
Asia	742,300
Africa	754,300
Europe-America	1,343,600
Non-Jews –Total	690,400
Moslems	530,800
Christians	94,000
Druze and other	65,600

(Percentages)

Jews	83.0
Moslems	13.1
Christians	2.3
Druze and other	1.6
JEWS – TOTAL	100.0
born in: Israel	15.8
Asia	22.0
Africa	22.4
Europe-America	39.8

Source: Statistical Abstract of Israel, 1983

BUDGET

Table 23.

GOVERNMENT REVENUE
(IS mn, current prices, budget years)

	1982/83	1983/84
Grand Total	**541,349**	**1,213,813**
Ordinary Budget – Total	385,500	840,500
Income Tax	143,600	270,490
Property Tax	1,400	1,760
Land Betterment Tax	1,850	6,340
V.A.T. Imposed on the Financial Sector	7,702	17,660
Employer's Tax	11,250	21,100
Customs-General	12,680	38,060
Customs-Fuel	4,310	9,550
Excise Duty	1,100	2,240
Value Added Tax	55,870	139,340
Purchase Tax	17,690	42,210
License Fees-Vehicles	588	2,300
-Other	1,442	2,370
Royalties from Enterprises and Natural Resources	1,618	171
Profits of the Bank of Israel	10,000	25,200
Interest	8,270	12,490
Refunds on Account of Former Years' Budgets	330	693
Income from Services	968	2,033
Transfer from Development Budget	104,732	214,703
Development Budget and Debt Repayment – Total	**106,000**	**214,500**

Source: Statistical Abstract of Israel, 1983

GOVERNMENT REVENUE
(IS million, at current prices; budget years)

	1982/83	1983/84
Foreign Sources: Development Loans		
External Loans and Grants	88,400	178,300
Internal Loans: from the National		
Insurance Institute	8,000	18,900
from Banks and Issues	58,000	164,500
Other revenue:		
Collections on Account of		
Loans and Sale of Property	4,000	4,075
Depreciation	146	345
Income o/a of Participation		
in Investments	8,377	12,273
Allowances for Pension and		
Severance Pay	815	1,712
Transfer to Ordinary Budget	-104,732	-214,703
Advances from the Bank of Israel	42,994	116,153
Commercial enterprises — Total	**49,849**	**90,813**
Treasury Projects	646	842
Housing Projects	10,074	15,096
Railways	853	1,838
Participation of Ordinary		
Budget in Railways' Expenditure	90	151
Communication Enterprises	19,520	39,841
Israel Lands Authority	4,928	10,500
Yafo Port	54	44
Israel Institute of Productivity	182	326
Institute for Teaching Aids	79	38
Government Trade Accounts	13,464	22,096

Table 24.

GOVERNMENT EXPENDITURE
(IS mn, current prices, budget years)

	1982/83	1983/84
Grand Total	541,349	1,213,813
Ordinary Budget — Total	385,500	840,500
President of the State, Knesset, Cabinet Ministers and State Comptroller	569	1,209
Prime Minister's Office	768	2,460
Ministry of:		
Immigrant Absorption	1,060	2,119
Finance	2,622	5,502
Defence	139,520	273,852
Health	9,029	21,200
Religious Affairs	2,262	4,667
Foreign Affairs	1,481	3,430
Education & Culture	34,500	72,367
Agriculture	1,160	2,701
Resettlement Grants to Settlers in Sinai	1,000	200
Industry & Trade	593	1,239
Tourism	240	530
Energy & Infrastructure	168	301
Economy & Interministerial Co-ordination	48	99
Interior	434	859
Police	6,720	14,062
Justice	962	2,079
Labour & Social Welfare	22,829	49,160
Construction & Housing	860	1,785
Transport	434	941
Science & Development		115
Financing Political Parties	120	305
Interest	71,000	195,500
Pensions & Compensations	5,614	12,380
Gratuities to Invalids	1,350	2,835
Transfer		
to Railways	90	151
to Transport	360	762
to Local Authorities	13,629	27,571

Source: Statistical Abstract of Israel, 1983

GOVERNMENT EXPENDITURE
(IS mn, current prices, budget years)

	1982/83	1983/84
Subsidies		
for Promotion of Exports	4,749	18,783
for Stabilization of Prices	24,000	47,565
Miscellaneous	872	2,822
Survey Department	58	118
Subsidies to Credit	20,000	33,200
Reserves	16,422	37,631
Development Budget and Debt		
Repayment — Total	**106,000**	**282,500**
Agriculture	3,468	6,492
Water projects	1,450	2,917
Industry and Trade	8,822	23,163
Tourism	1,810	3,591
Transport and Roads	1,459	3,108
Communication	2,400	5,040
Housing	11,000	22,370
Loans to Local Authorities	880	1,716
Buildings for Public and Government		
Institutions and Investments		
in Social Services	3,367	7,031
Development of Energy Sources	2,060	2,783
Debt Repayment	66,000	193,500
National Council of Research		
and Development		100
Reserve	2,633	7,614
Budgetary Working Capital	88	185
Business Enterprises — Total	**49,849**	**90,813**
Treasury Projects	646	842
Housing Projects	10,074	15,096
Railways	943	1,989
Communication Enterprises	19,520	39,841
Israel Lands Authority	4,928	10,500
Yafo Port	54	44
Israel Institute of Productivity	182	326
Institute for Teaching Aids	38	79
Government Trade Accounts	13,464	22,096

Average annual percentage of change in general government consumption per capita (at fixed prices — 1976-1981): -1.7%

Table 25.

GOVERNMENT REVENUES 1984/1985 COMPARED TO 1983/84
(IS mn)

	1983/84	1984/85	Change %
Taxes	16,980	17,600	+ 3.7
Income Taxes	9,370	8,360	- 10.8
Purchase Taxes	9,120	4,600	- 11.5
Domestic Loans	4,250	3,760	+ 75.5
Foreign Loans & Grants	2,370	4,160	- 9.8
Income from Property	570	540	- 5.2
Money Printing	1,090	1,310	+ 20.2

Source: Israeli Economist, May, 1984

Table 26.

GOVERNMENT DEBT, BY TYPE
(IS million, at current prices) /1

	1975	1980	1981	1982
Total	9,362	105,468	322,574	811,294
Internal Debt- Total	6,207	58,956	224,748	559,361
Linked to Foreign Currency /2	451	5,327	5,024	38,793
CPI Linked	5,397	52,202	218,388	517,966
Non-linked	359	1,427	1,336	2,602
External Debt	3,155	46,512	97,826	251,933
Repayable in IS	73	226	428	814
Repayable in Foreign Currency /3	3,082	46,286	97,398	251,119

/1 Excluding current liabilities
/2 Adjusted to changes in the rate of exchange or the CPI
/3 Value calculated according to the rate of exchange on 31 March each
   year

Source: Statistical Abstract of Israel, 1983

ENERGY

Table 27.

ENERGY SUPPLY AND DEMAND
(Thousand T.O.E.)

	1978	1979	1980	1981	1982
Production					
Total	7,443	7,784	7,864	8,038	8,345
Petroleum Refining	- 532	- 548	- 578	- 542	- 594
Electricity Generation	-1,738	-1,822	-1,840	-1,897	-1,942
Consumption					
Total	5,053	5,280	5,319	5,450	5,650
Industry	1,532	1,662	1,712	--	--
Agriculture	213	165	155	--	--
Water	169	29	28	--	--
Transportation	1,445	1,506	1,405	--	--
Private and Commercial	1,530	1,622	1,752	--	--

Source: Statistical Abstract of Israel, 1983

Table 28.

PRODUCTION AND SUPPLY OF ELECTRICITY
BY THE ISRAEL ELECTRIC CORPORATION

Year	Installed Capacity (megawatts)	Annual Peak Load (megawatts)	Generation (million KWH)	Number of Consumers
1950	100	110	543	203,000
1960	410	420	2,205	551,000
1965	720	720	4,061	759,000
1970	1,226	1,115	6,610	912,000
1975	2,181	1,509	9,349	1,103,000
1980	2,737	2,070	12,089	1,271,000
1981	3,032	2,160	12,677	1,297,000
1982	3,402	2,240	13,363	1,318,000

Source: Statistical Abstract of Israel, 1983

able 29.

PETROLEUM PRODUCT PRICES
(January, 1982)

Price per gallon in U.S. Dollars)

Premium gasoline 94 RON	2.08
Regular gasoline 83 RON	1.84
Auto diesel fuel	1.49
Household kerosene	1.37
Light heating oil	1.13
LPG	1.18

Price per barrel in U.S. Dollars)

Distillate fuel oil	58.88
Marine Diesel fuel	45.58
Medium tuel oil	38.48
Heavy fuel oil	33.93
Marine fuel oil	29.14

ource: International Energy Annual, 1983

able 30.

FUEL PRODUCTS (1972-82)
(Shekels per ton in 1972 prices)

	Petrol	Heavy Crude	Diesel	Kerosene
972	89.4	7.7	22.3	31.3
973	87.9	7.0	24.5	34.3
974	134.7	14.7	41.1	56.1
975	156.5	21.6	54.9	70.1
976	161.2	21.6	55.2	70.9
977	157.5	23.0	49.7	63.9
978	152.6	26.8	53.9	62.3
979	171.9	28.1	56.6	65.0
980	198.5	38.0	69.9	80.2
981	164.3	46.1	90.1	103.1
982	162.2	46.7	108.1	127.2
increase 1972-82	81.4	506.5	384.8	307.0

ource: International Energy Annual, 1983

Table 31.

WATER CONSUMPTION BY USE
(mn cubic meters)

	1977/78	1978/79	1979/80	1980/81
Domestic	348	367	375	367
Industrial	94	96	90	100
Agriculture	1,231	1,327	1,235	1,212

Source: Statistical Abstract of Israel, 1983

Table 32.

OUTPUT OF REFINED PETROLEUM PRODUCTS, 1980
(thousand barrels per day)

Motor Gasoline	20
Total Gasoline (including aviation gasoline)	24
Jet Fuel	12
Distillate Fuel Oil	31
Residual Fuel Oil	53
Lubricants	1
Refinery Fuel and Loss	11
Total Output of Refined Petroleum Products	152

Source: 1981 International Energy Annual

INDUSTRY AND AGRICULTURE

Table 33.

PRODUCTION OF INDUSTRIAL PRODUCTS

Product (Unit)	1980	1981	1982
Mining and Quarrying			
Crude oil (mn l)	23	18	15
Natural gas (mn cu m)	142	175	73
Potash (1,000 tons)	1,343	1,332	1,694
Phosphate rock (1,000 tons)	2,307	1,919	2,148
Food			
Flour (1,000 tons)			
Standard	97	92	95
Other	358	372	403
Milk products			
Pasteurized Milk (mn l)	187.3	205	218.4
Sterilized Milk (1,000 l)	17,305	19,889	23,460
Cream (tons)	10,208	12,299	14,200
Soft Cheese (tons)	39,447	42,331	44,775
Hard Cheese (tons)	9,747	11,471	13,100
Yoghurt, Sour and			
Skimmed Milk (tons)	57,411	66,507	69,032
Sugar			
Refined Sugar (tons)	---	8,800	---
Molasses (tons)	---	8,100	---
Oils (tons)			
Margarine	33,622	32,899	33,914
Refined Oils	67,665	68,143	78,300
Alcoholic Beverages (1,000 l)			
Wine (marketing)	18,896	16,643	16,026
Beer (except malt)	39,437	43,876	40,190
Arrack, Brandy, Other Spirits	5,749	5,575	4,922
Tobacco Products			
Cigarettes (tons)	5,337	5,985	6,043
Cigars (kg)	9,078	7,399	3,319
Pipe Tobacco (kg)	8,295	5,550	1,230
Tombac (kg)	41,285	31,670	35,291
Snuff (kg)	27,349	24,408	23,808
Textiles			
Cotton yarn (tons)	20,013	17,266	16,518
Combed wool yarn (tons)	5,354	4,228	3,706
Carded wool yarn (tons)	2,251	2,842	2,751

Source: Statistical Abstract of Israel 1983

PRODUCTION OF INDUSTRIAL PRODUCTS

roduct (Unit)	1980	1981	1982
ood			
Plywood (cubic m)	96,885	87,790	91,345
aper and Cardboard (tons)			
Newsprint	4,548	5,590	3,274
Writing and printing paper	59,894	60,005	54,776
Other paper	23,541	30,161	27,202
Cardboard	36,023	40,670	43,529
ubber Products			
Tires (1,000)	1,242	1,106	1,087
(tons)	32,141	29,166	31,134
Inner Tubes (1,000)	455	401	439
(tons)	1,209	973	1,227
hemicals			
Ammonia (tons)	66,702	52,340	95,209
Ammonium Sulphate (tons)	38,231	31,224	28,219
Potassium Sulphate (tons)	12,001	9,937	11,621
Ethylene Gas (tons)	4,278	1,221	---
Di-calcium Phosphate (tons)	16,466	12,036	15,203
Sulphuric Acid (100%) (1,000 tons)	209	182	154
Chlorine (tons)	35,310	34,131	30,210
Caustic Soda (tons)	35,268	34,553	29,346
Sodium Hypochlorite (tons)	14,348	11,225	11,073
Polyethylene (tons)	60,597	48,016	66,597
Potassium Carbonate (tons)	4,675	4,647	4,998
Paraffin (tons)	5,718	3,977	4,519
Paints (tons)	26,953	31,380	31,478
Synthetic Detergents			
− Powder (tons)	26,069	24,914	---
on-metallic Mineral Products			
Glazed Tiles (1000)	44,094	50,677	49,239
Cement (1000 tons)	2,092	2,361	2,189
lectrical Equipment			
Electricity Meters	16,774	33,663	32,014
Accumulators	321.6	327.8	306.5
ransport Equipment			
Passenger Cars	1,649	786	---
Commercial Vehicles	2,329	2,797	2,494

156

Table 34.

INDEX OF INDUSTRIAL PRODUCTION
(1978=100)

1958	15.7
1968	48.1
1970	61.0
1975	85.2
1976	88.9
1977	94.6
1978	100.0
1979	105.2
1980	102.0
1981	108.4
1982	109.1

Source: Statistical Abstract of Israel, 1983

Table 35.

ESTABLISHMENTS AND EMPLOYED PERSONS BY TYPE
(minimum of 5 employees)

Type	Employed Persons (thousands)	Establishments
Single Owner	11.2	1,258
Partnership	9.8	1,009
Private Company	142.3	3,330
Public Company	74.2	157
Co-operative	15.5	299
Other	14.5	26

Source: Statistical Abstract of Israel, 1983

Table 36.

TOURISTS ARRIVING, BY COUNTRY OF RESIDENCE

	1981	1982
Grand Total	1,137,056	997,510
Asia-Total	36,131	51,633
Turkey and Cyprus	11,963	8,838
Japan	3,339	3,911
Africa-Total	28,511	30,156
Union of South Africa	17,646	18,443
Other	10,865	7,544
Europe-Total	709,786	576,299
Scandinavia	65,233	52,061
United Kingdom	143,185	126,768
Netherlands	32,244	28,880
Belgium	20,197	15,735
France	147,960	129,612
Spain	10,991	7,785
Italy	49,176	35,113
Switzerland	31,424	29,290
Germany, F.R.	155,087	107,446
Austria	22,925	16,835
Rumania	3,458	3,289
Yugoslavia	1,795	1,234
Greece	10,795	11,188
America-Total	343,947	324,991
Canada	27,825	26,591
U.S.A.	270,852	263,495
Mexico	12,630	6,275
Argentina	13,510	7,372
Brazil	7,475	8,222
Uruguay	1,514	2,111
Chile	1,578	1,750
Oceania-Total	14,549	14,431
Australia	12,112	11,633
New Zealand	2,283	1,967

Source: Statistical Abstract of Israel, 1983

Table 37.

CULTIVATED AREA
(thousand dunams)

	1978/79	1979/80	1980/81	1981/82
Total	4,270	4,270	4,200	4,100
Irrigated	1,890	2,030	2,030	2,030
Field Crops	2,806	2,800	2,747	2,595
Vegetables and Melons	357	355	335	334
Citrus	402	396	411	407
Fruit Plantations (excluding citrus)	474	490	480	534
Fish Ponds	41	39	37	40
Afforested Area	658	678	691	708
Other	190	190	190	190

Source: Statistical Abstract of Israel, 1983

Table 38.

CONSUMPTION OF FERTILIZERS IN AGRICULTURE
(tons)

	1980/81	1981/82	1982/83
Plant Nutrients			
Nitrogen	39,200	35,500	39,200
Phosphate	14,700	14,500	13,800
Potash	21,900	22,900	19,450
Fertilizers			
Ammonium Sulphate	54,100	46,700	52,500
Ammonium Nitrate	50,200	51,900	49,500
Urea	15,400	11,400	15,500
Aqua Ammonia	41,530	36,400	40,500
Potassium Sulphate	100	100	180
Muriate	32,100	33,400	27,400

Source: Statistical Abstract of Israel, 1983

Table 39.

INDEX OF AGRICULTURAL PRODUCTION
(1967/66=100)

1977/78	171
1978/79	177
1979/80	179
1980/81	189
1981/82	203

Source: Statistical Abstract of Israel

Table 40.

AGRICULTURAL AREA AND NUMBER OF LANDHOLDERS BY TYPE OF FARM
(1980-1981)

	Israel Land Administration	Private Ownership
Area		
Non-Jewish Farms	33,497	444,235
Jewish Farms	4,706,094	138,751
Private Farmers	335,549	107,558
Moshavim	1,777,881	20,899
Collective Moshavim	293,728	100
Quibbuzim	2,298,936	10,194
Grand Total	4,739,591	582,986
Number of Holders		
Non-Jewish Farms	1,018	13,252
Jewish Farms	31,794	2,475
Private Farmers	3,425	1,991
Moshavim	28,063	444
Collective Moshavim	44	0
Quibbuzim	262	0
Grand Total	32,812	15,709

Source: Statistical Abstract of Israel, 1983

Table 41.
VOLUME OF AGRICULTURAL PRODUCTION
ALL FARMS 1980/81
(figures in thousand tons, unless otherwise stated)

Field Crops

Cereals and pulses for grains	268.6
Wheat	215.0
Barley	20.4
Sorghum	10.2
Industrial and oil crops	391.2
Cotton Lint	94.8
Cotton Seed	152.0
Sugar Beet	98.1
Groundnuts	25.5
Canning Peas	5.8
Hay	112.0
Green Fodder and Silage	1,117.9
Straw	177.7
Vegetables, Potatoes, and Melons	1,027.2
Vegetables	676.5
Tomatoes	283.3
Cucumbers	50.8
Carrots	50.1
Peppers and Gamba	48.8
Dry onions	53.8
Eggplants	27.6
Cabbage	35.3
Beets, Red	9.1
Celery	6.7
Potatoes	218.1
Water melons	87.0
Sugar melons	45.6
Citrus	1,421.1
Shamouti	536.4
Lates	248.8
Grapefruit	494.0
Lemons	51.7
Other	90.2

Source: Statistical Abstract of Israel, 1983

VOLUME OF AGRICULTURAL PRODUCTION
ALL FARMS 1980/81
(figures in thousand tons, unless otherwise stated)

ruit, Excluding Citrus	427.3
Apples	129.0
Pears	19.5
Peaches	40.2
Apricots	13.0
Plums	21.1
Table Grapes	43.9
Wine Grapes	39.8
Bananas	65.8
Olives	19.7
lowers, Exports(millions)	
Roses	116.4
Carnations	260.8
ilk	725.9
Cow's milk	682.0
Sheep's milk	20.8
Goat's milk	23.1
ggs and Chicks (millions)	
Table eggs	1,349.0
Chicks	110.6
ish	23.1
Pond culture	11.8
Lake catch	1.8
Marine catch	9.5
ivestock for Meat	266.3
Poultry	209.8
Broilers	143.9
Turkeys	54.2
Layers and others	11.7
Cattle	35.4
Sheep	5.8
Goats	2.7

Table 42.
LIVESTOCK POPULATION-JEWISH FARMS
(1981/82)

Cattle	299,000
Dairy cattle	
Cows	108,000
Heifers and calves	81,750
Bulls	250
Beef Cattle	102,000
Poultry	
Laying hens	8,600,000
Broilers	17,900,000
Turkeys, geese and ducks	6,800,000
Sheep and Goats	
Sheep	90,000
Goats, improved breed	16,000
Beehives	65,000

Source: Statistical Abstract of Israel, 1983

TRADE

Table 43.

FOREIGN TRADE INDICATORS

Average annual growth rate, imports (1976-1981): 14.0%
Average annual growth rate, exports (1976-1981): 18.2%

	1977	1978	1979	1980	1981
Ratio of exports to GDP	22.4	28.9	26.0	27.2	26.4
Ratio of imports to GDP	42.0	55.2	50.0	48.0	---
Ratio of exports to imports	.53	.52	.52	.57	---
Terms of trade	111.9	120.1	112.0	102.7	102.2

Source: International Financial Statistics Trade Supplement

Table 44.

BALANCE OF FOREIGN TRADE(1981)
(Does not include trade with Judaea, Samaria, Gaza, Sinai)
(mn $)

Gross Imports	7,992.8
Returned Imports	145.6
Net Imports	7,847.2
Gross Exports	5,664.2
Returned Exports	341.2
Net Exports	5,323.0
Excess of imports over exports	2,524.2
Exports as % of imports	67.8
Imports per capita	1,986.0
Exports per capita	1,347.0
Trade deficit	639.0

Source: Statistical Abstract of Israel, 1982

able 45.

BALANCE OF PAYMENTS
($ mn)

	1979	1980	1981	1982	1983
xports fob	4,759	5,799	5,906	5,560	5,511
mports fob	-7,923	-8,981	-9,410	-8,857	-8,691
xports of Services	3,271	3,993	4,538	4,552	4,435
mports of Services	-3,764	-4,586	-5,389	-6,079	-6,294
et Transfers					
Private	951	1,006	1,148	984	923
Goverment	1,842	1,960	1,782	1,632	1,939
urrent Account Balance	-864	-809	-1,425	-2,208	-2,177
irect Investment	10	-84	26	13	48
ortfolio Investment	-29	72	-69	55	646
ther Long-term Capital	1,280	1,196	1,190	1,138	1,470
hort-term Capital	485	38	917	1,591	-511
et Errors and Omissions	-672	127	-88	276	452
otal Change in Reserves	-508	-387	-385	-543	473

ource: IMF International Financial Statistics, 1983

able 46.

DIRECTION OF TRADE
(% of total)

Exports(1981)

Industrial Countries	67.8
Oil Exporting Countries	1.3
Non-Oil Developing Countries	14.9
Other Countries	16.0

Imports(1981)

Industrial Countries	57.3
Oil Exporting Countries	--
Non-oil Developing Countries	5.4
Other Countries	37.3

ource: International Financial Statistics Supplement on Trade

Table 47.

EXPORTS BY ECONOMIC SECTOR
(mn $)

	1981	1982
Grand Total	**5,670.1**	**5,281.5**
Agricultural Total	599.6	553.0
Citrus Fruit	246.3	185.6
Other	353.3	367.4
Industry Total	4,945.3	4,606.2
Mining and Quarrying	194.4	189.1
Food, Beverages and Tobacco	333.6	332.4
Textiles	109.7	92.5
Clothing and Made-up Articles	277.0	255.4
Leather and Leather Products	8.4	6.5
Wood and Wood Products	27.7	22.9
Paper and Paper Products	7.6	6.4
Printing and Publishing	20.7	19.9
Rubber and Plastic Products	107.7	107.2
Chemical and Oil Products	653.0	580.1
Non-metallic Mineral Products	17.1	14.5
Basic Metal	58.6	35.5
Metal Products	463.6	514.6
Machinery	116.6	112.0
Electrical and Electronic Equipment	387.1	465.7
Transport Equipment	513.3	439.9
Diamonds, Polished -Gross	1,397.1	1,157.7
-Net	1,067.2	904.7
Miscellaneous	252.1	253.9
Other Exports Total	125.2	122.3
Returned Exports	-341.2	- 264.7
Net Exports ⁻ Total	**5,328.9**	**5,016.8**

Source: Statistical Abstract of Israel, 1983

able 48.

IMPORTS BY ECONOMIC USE
(Figures in US $ million)

	1981	1982
rand Total	7,992.6	8,116.1
onsumer Goods or Direct Consumption-Total	756.4	832.0
Non-durables	451.3	472.9
Food	313.4	296.3
Other	137.9	176.6
Durables	305.1	359.1
roduction Inputs-Total	6,191.9	5,975.1
Agriculture	272.2	233.0
Diamonds -Gross	609.0	641.1
-Net	529.1	571.8
Fuel and Lubricants	2,043.2	1,914.2
Spare Parts, Accessories, Tools	659.7	697.6
Production Inputs, Other	2,607.8	2,489.2
nvestment Goods Total	1,037.0	1,295.1
Machines, Equipment, Implements and Accessories	810.3	996.6
Transport Equipment	226.7	298.5
Ships and Aircraft	69.3	70.3
oods, N.E.S. Total	7.3	13.9
eturned Imports	-145.6	-155.7
et Imports Total	7,847.0	7,960.4

ource: Statistical Abstract of Israel, 1983

Table 49.
IMPORTS, BY COUNTRY OF PURCHASE AND EXPORTS, BY COUNTRY OF DESTINATION (1982)
(US $ million)

Country	Exports	Imports
Grand Total	**5,281.5**	**8,116.1**
Europe (Total)	2,227.3	3,854.1
Common Market	1,751.2	2,999.1
Italy	202.3	441.9
Ireland	16.5	10.2
Belgium & Luxembourg	232.2	367.5
Germany, F.R	366.9	895.2
Denmark	18.0	33.7
Netherlands	199.4	248.3
United Kingdom	417.0	618.8
Greece	40.3	18.8
France	258.6	364.7
Free Trade Area	337.5	701.1
Austria	37.4	38.6
Iceland	0.3	0.5
Norway	20.4	10.1
Portugal	58.1	14.7
Finland	21.7	50.7
Sweden	41.4	101.1
Switzerland	158.2	485.4
Other Countries of Europe	138.6	153.9
Bulgaria	6.6	11.6
U.S.S.R.	0.0	0.0
Hungary	4.6	8.1
Turkey	26.3	14.4
Yugoslavia	25.1	30.2
Spain	28.6	42.1
Cyprus	15.1	2.7
Rumania	24.2	44.6
Asia (Total)	528.9	301.4
India	3.1	17.6
Hongkong	179.8	39.0

Source: Statistical Abstract of Israel, 1983

IMPORTS, BY COUNTRY OF PURCHASE AND EXPORTS, BY COUNTRY OF DESTINATION (1982)
(US $ million)

Country	Exports	Imports
Asia (cont.)		
Japan	193.4	186.3
Singapore	40.4	14.9
Other	112.1	43.6
Africa (Total)	190.2	191.8
Ethiopia	4.1	4.0
Gabon	0.8	10.0
Ghana	0.6	0.3
South Africa	78.4	166.8
Ivory Coast	2.7	7.1
Tanzania	4.3	0.5
Liberia	0.1	---
Nigeria	43.3	0.0
Kenya	14.4	2.2
America (Total)	1,282.6	1,810.3
North America	1,160.3	1,656.5
U.S.A.	1,119.2	1,542.0
Mexico	8.0	2.1
Canada	33.1	112.4
Central America	13.7	1.7
Guatemala	3.8	0.2
Panama	4.2	0.6
South America	108.6	152.1
Uruguay	1.3	15.6
Argentina	12.2	59.4
Brazil	19.7	60.4
Venezuela	21.3	0.9
Peru	8.2	1.8
Colombia	13.3	4.1
Oceania (Total)	69.8	50.5
Australia	64.0	49.9
New Zealand	5.7	0.6
Unclassified Countries	898.8	1,908.0

Table 50.

EXPORTS BY DESTINATION AND IMPORTS BY ORIGIN
(mn $)

	1983 (Jan)	1983 III	1983 IV	1984 (Jan)
EXPORTS				
World	392.7	1,036.1	1,493.8	443.3
Industrial Countries	277.2	757.8	1,081.5	306.9
Oil Exporting Countries	2.7	9.2	12.9	4.7
Nigeria	2.4	8.0	11.0	4.3
Venezuela	.3	1.2	1.9	.4
Non-Oil Developing	62.2	150.1	206.4	56.5
Africa	9.3	30.0	37.9	15.3
Asia	29.0	71.9	90.8	18.1
Europe	15.4	25.6	51.5	18.0
Egypt	1.9	.8	1.1	1.1
Western Hemisphere	6.6	21.8	25.1	4.0
USSR and Eastern Europe	2.8	1.4	2.4	1.6
IMPORTS				
World	761.2	2,306.7	2,232.5	660.1
Industrial Countries	519.1	1,573.9	1,600.0	524.9
Oil Exporting Countries	--	--	1.0	--
Nigeria	--	--	1.0	--
Venezuela	--	--	--	--
Non-Oil Developing	44.7	134.4	134.4	35.1
Africa	10.5	45.5	48.6	10.1
Asia	10.2	24.1	22.0	5.6
Europe	12.3	28.4	27.5	10.3
Egypt	--	1.3	1.2	--
Western Hemisphere	11.7	35.1	34.7	9.1
USSR and Eastern Europe	.9	4.5	3.0	.1

Source: IMF Direction of Trade, June 1984

LABOR

Table 51.
EMPLOYED PERSONS, BY ECONOMIC SECTOR, AND SEX
(1982)

	Total	Males	Females
Agriculture, Forestry, and Fishing	5.7%	7.1%	3.1%
Industry (Mining and Manufacturing)	22.9%	28.0%	13.9%
Electricity and Water	1.1%	1.5%	0.3%
Construction (Building and Public Works)	6.2%	9.3%	0.9%
Commerce, Restaurants and Hotels	12.1%	12.4%	11.7%
Transport, Storage and Communication	6.8%	8.6%	3.8%
Financing and Business Services	9.0%	7.4%	11.9%
Public and Community Services	30.1%	20.7%	46.3%
Personal and Other Services	6.1%	5.0%	8.1%

Total number of employed persons (1982): 1,298,300
Percent Jews of total employed persons (1982): 89.6%
Percent women of total employed persons (1982): 36.1%
Annual growth rate of civilian labor force (1976-1981): 2.9%
Civilian labor force (1982): 1,366,700
Percent unemployed of civilian labor torce (1982): 5.0%

Source: Statistical Abstract of Israel, 1983

Table 52.
EMPLOYED PERSONS BY OCCUPATION

Skill Level	% of Employed Persons
Scientific and academic workers	8.2%
Other professional, technical, and related workers	14.9%
Administrators and managers	3.7%
Clerical and related workers	18.9%
Sales workers	7.6%
Service workers	11.2%
Agricultural workers	5.5%
Skilled workers in industry, mining, building, transport, and other skilled workers	25.8%
Other workers in industry, transport, building, and unskilled workers	4.2%
	100.0%

Source: Statistical Abstract of Israel, 1983

TRANSPORTATION AND COMMUNICATION

Table 53.

TRANSPORTATION AND COMMUNICATIONS INFRASTRUCTURE
(1982)

Length of Road	12,360
Length of Railway (km)	536
Tonnage Transported (000)	5,338
Passengers (000)	2,838
Ships	
Arriving (no.)	3,111
Tonnage of Ships Arriving (000 NRT)	10,915
Freight loaded (000 tons)	6,219
Freight unloaded	6,348
Passenger traffic (000)	259
Air Transport	
Passengers Traffic (000)	2,748
Telephones (000)	1,380
Telex (no.)	4,300

Source: Statistical Abstract of Israel, 1983

Table 54.

MOTOR VEHICLES, BY TYPE OF VEHICLES

	1965	1970	1975	1980	1981
TOTAL	171,309	266,233	419,389	532,430	592,916
Private cars	80,542	147,785	279,486	405,007	453,634
Taxi cabs	2,604	3,420	4,542	4,869	5,544
Trucks	41,541	66,013	96,138	87,569	96,145
Buses	3,247	4,655	5,770	7,062	7,691
Special Service Vehicles	1,377	2,325	3,302	3,032	3,438
Motorcycles and motor scooters	42,138	42,035	30,148	24,891	26,464

Source: Statistical Abstract of Israel, 1983

Table 55.

PRINCIPAL DAILY NEWSPAPERS

Al-Anba	Hatzofeh	Sha'ar
Al-Fajr	Israel Nachrichten	Shearim
Al Hamishmar	Israelski Far Tribuna	Uj Kelet
Al Quds	Jerusalem Post	Viata Noastra
Al Sha'ab	Le Journal d'Israel	Yedioth Aharonoth
Hadshot Hasport	Letzte Nyess	Yom Yom
Davar	Ma'ariv	
Ha'aretz	Nowiny i Kurier	
Hamodia	Omer	

HEALTH, EDUCATION AND WELFARE

Table 56.

HEALTH CARE FACILITIES AND PERSONNEL
(1982)

Total	145

Type

General Care	43
Mental Diseases	37
Chronic Diseases	62
Rehabilitation	3

Ownership

Government	34
Municipal Government	2
Local Authorities	1
General Workers Sick Fund	14
Hadassah	1
Missions	7
Other Non-profit Hospitals	31
Private Hospitals	55

Source: Statistical Abstract of Israel, 1983

Table 57.

EDUCATIONAL INSTITUTIONS
(1982/83)

Total	2,437
Hebrew Education	2,035
Primary Schools- Total	1,491
Schools for Handicapped	1,277
Intermediate Schools	253
Secondary Schools	499
Other	
General	267
Continuation	56
Vocational	301
Agricultural	26
Arab Education	402
Primary Schools	330
Schools for Handicapped	15
Intermediate Schools	50
Secondary Schools	73
Other	
General	57
Vocational	36
Agricultural	2

Source: Statistical Abstract of Israel, 1983

Table 58.

EDUCATIONAL ENROLLMENT
(1980/1981)

Total Enrollment	1,306,651
Hebrew Education	
Teaching Posts	
Primary Education	38,886
Intermediate Schools	10,824
Secondary Education	19,620
Teacher Training Colleges	3,300
Pupils	936,300
Kindergartens	254,480
Primary Education	471,197
Intermediate Schools	87,873
Secondary Education	159,354
Other	
General	70,310
Continuation	7,438
Vocational	76,636
Agricultural	4,970
Teacher Training Colleges	11,492
Universities	62,000
Arab Education	
Teaching Posts	
Primary Education	6,602
Intermediate Schools	1,267
Secondary Education	1,650
Teacher Training Colleges	100
Pupils	200,921
Kindergartens	18,652
Primary education	135,317
Intermediate schools	18,091
Secondary education	28,326
Other	
General	23,679
Vocational	3,953
Agricultural	694
Teacher training colleges	365

Source: Statistical Abstract of Israel, 1983

Table 59.

FAMILIES RECEIVING MATERIAL ASSISTANCE FROM WELFARE BUREAU
(% of total families)

Type of Need	Non-Jewish	Jewish	Total
Old Age	1.4	2.0	1.9
Invalidity or Chronic Disease	61.6	43.1	45.9
Blindness	1.2	1.5	1.4
Mental Illness	3.7	4.1	4.1
Widow with Children	19.0	26.3	25.2
Unemployable	1.6	2.9	2.7
Low Income	3.5	11.8	10.6
Other	8.0	8.3	8.2
Total Expenditure (IS thousands current prices)	3,534	19,954	23,448

Source: Statistical Abstract of Israel, 1983

For Product Safety Concerns and Information please contact our EU
representative GPSR@taylorandfrancis.com Taylor & Francis Verlag GmbH,
Kaufingerstraße 24, 80331 München, Germany

Printed and bound by CPI Group (UK) Ltd, Croydon, CR0 4YY

08/05/2025

01864379-0004